D0368927

RELATING TO LEARNING

Relating to Learning

Towards a Developmental Social Psychology of the Primary School

PETER KUTNICK

Lecturer in Education, University of Sussex

London
GEORGE ALLEN & UNWIN

Boston   Sydney

George Allen & Unwin (Publishers) Ltd,
40 Museum Street, London WC1A 1LU, UK

George Allen & Unwin (Publishers) Ltd,
Park Lane, Hemel Hempstead, Herts HP2 4TE, UK

Allen & Unwin, Inc.,
9 Winchester Terrace, Winchester, Mass. 01890, USA

George Allen & Unwin Australia Pty Ltd,
8 Napier Street, North Sydney, NSW 2060, Australia

First published in 1983

British Library Cataloguing in Publication Data

Kutnick, Peter
    Relating to learning: towards a developmental
social psychology of the primary school.—
(Unwin education books)
1. Education, Primary   2. Learning, Psychology
I. Title
370.1'52   LB1513   OLSON LIBRARY
ISBN 0-04-370137-X
ISBN 0-04-370138-8 Pbk NORTHERN MICHIGAN UNIVERSITY
                        MARQUETTE, MICHIGAN   49855

Library of Congress Cataloging in Publication Data

Kutnick, Peter.
    Relating to learning.
(Unwin education books)
Bibliography: p.
Includes index.
1. Education, Elementary – Social aspects.
2. Socialization.   3. School environment.   I. Title.
II. Series.
LC210.K87 1983   372.18   83-8781
ISBN 0-04-370137-X
ISBN 0-04-370138-8 (pbk.)

Set in 10 on 11 point Times by Rowland Phototypesetting Ltd
Bury St Edmunds, Suffolk
and printed in Great Britain
by Billing and Sons Ltd, London and Worcester

Contents

To Sam

Preface

The following chapters have been written and presented by the author with two objectives: to expand and apply current research, theory and practice concerning the growing child; and to gain greater insight concerning the realities and possibilities developed in the child's interactions with, and in the context of, the primary school. This book is written from a strongly cognitive developmental (psychological) perspective (most elaborately presented by Jean Piaget's early research and writings), concerning the social, moral and intellectual development of the child. The opening chapters set a brief theoretical background to development. Later chapters present research results concerning the social development of primary-school-aged children. The research results are derived from in-depth interviews and observations of over 175 children from four schools, along with interviews with their teachers, heads, and so on. The closing chapters bring the separate findings of the research together, expand upon relevant theory and suggest applications of the findings to the structuring of primary schools.

In discussing the development of the child, the term 'development' must include cognitive/intellectual, social and affective aspects. Cognitive/intellectual development is a subject well covered by Piaget (see Piaget and Inhelder, 1969) and much explored, expanded and criticised in today's fields of developmental and educational psychology. Research into cognitive development presents the child as an active organiser of the environment, who uses various methods or schemes to adapt to it. Social development is a relatively new field and covers multiple topics, centring on concepts of self and others, and on interpersonal and moral relationships. It is a vitally important aspect of development as it underlies and characterises the child's adaptive relationship to the environment. The affective aspect is undoubtedly the most difficult to define; yet it too is vital to development. Affect may best be understood as the realisation and expression of emotion. Emotions are most often generated in scenes or situations between people; affect is interpersonal. Affect is initially characterised in the trust and dependence between a child and caretaker, laying the foundation for the development of close interpersonal relationships of love. Close relationships, as will be discussed in this book, are essential for further moral and social developments. While cognitive, social and affective aspects of development have been introduced separately, research in this book explores how the aspects are combined, thus supporting an early Piagetian contention that the aspects are 'intertwined'. A theoretical and practical overview of development will be described in Chapters 1 and 2.

Development has been described as an example of adaptation. The environment to which the child adapts must also be explored. Research into effects of the home have provided preliminary data on the aspects of development. In order to understand more fully the child's 'integration' into the social world, a further institution which draws the child beyond the home must be explored. The institution to which most children (in the West) have immediate access is the school. The primary school is of utmost importance; its role is to promote intellectual and social development (discussed in Chapter 3). In so doing the primary school is tied to and relies upon the child's affective development (explored in the research chapters). It is not simply the process of entering school that provides a context which promotes development. The child and other actors in the school form relationships which characterise and structure the 'learning experience' of the school.

The study reported in this volume notes the above qualifications concerning development and the context within which it takes place. The study focuses on the underlying schemes of authority development. Parts of the study show children's behavioural interaction with school authority, understanding of this authority and schemes of adapting to the social/school context. In a practical sense, the study traces the primary school child's introduction to and interaction with school and peers. In a broader sense, the study also approaches theoretical issues of authority and moral development which intertwine aspects of cognition, affect and social understanding of relationships. Approaching the theoretical issue also involves a firm methodological stance which brings together observational and interview procedures set to explore development, while also noting the limitations and effects of the school context (see further discussion in Chapter 4).

The fifth chapter reports the empirical and statistical results of the individual parts of the study concerning classroom behaviour and corresponding knowledge. The end of the chapter brings together several aspects of authority development found in the study. A model of stages in social authority is constructed from the data. The methodological and empirical reportage of the fourth and fifth chapters will be of particular interest to those readers involved in educational and social (including psychological) research. Chapter 6 begins with a general summary of the results from the study. Theoretical and practical constraints on development are discussed. Implications and extensions for school/social development are discussed using the research findings and the theoretical model. Among the conclusions and recommendations a restructuring of teaching style within the context of the present-day curriculum is discussed, with reference to the perception of knowledge and authority, competence and the classroom peer group.

Acknowledgements

The writing of this book has had a long history of support from friends, colleagues and relatives – too numerous to name. Perhaps the deepest support was drawn from my parents who raised me in an atmosphere of independence and responsibility. My initial studies were encouraged by John Versey. A most supportive and co-operative environment in which to live was created by those who were part of Melrose. My deepest appreciation goes to Carole, who encouraged, supported and debated with me; she also read and corrected the draft and made it possible for me to complete it. I would also like to thank my colleagues and acquaintances on both sides of the Atlantic and the secretarial staff who helped with the draft.

My thanks also go to William Damon and Robert Selman for their permission to reprint their developmental tables of Early Authority Levels and Social-Perspective-Taking (pp. 28–9 and 31–2).

Chapter 1

Introduction and Review of Early Development of the Child

Early development in children has often been characterised in terms of either social or cognitive development with some underlying reference to emotion (or affect). A major purpose of this book is to demonstrate how these aspects of development are intertwined within the context of the primary school. Research and reviews cited in this chapter are brought together to set a background of development within the theoretical perspective of the book. A further purpose of this chapter is to introduce simple observational and interview findings for greater depth of developmental understanding: an understanding that shows the intertwining of cognition, social and affective developments.

The following are naturalistic observations of four children in an infant school. Each observation was made over a period of a few minutes, recording as much information about the child as possible and making a minimum of inferences.

The first observation is of a 4-year-old male, made in a continuous three-minute period during classroom activities.

H went to the toy cupboard, took out a box of coloured animal shapes, sorted approximately ten animals into piles (classified by colour), put the animals back into the box and the box back into the cupboard. He then sat on a wooden train and pushed himself halfway around the room avoiding furniture and people while saying in quiet tones: 'Choo, choo, train coming. Watch out!' He transferred on to a flat board with wheels and pushed himself around another quarter of the room, looked up at his teacher, smiled and put the top (that had previously fallen off) back on a toy. He looked towards the climbing bars where four other children were playing. He went over to the paint easel, looked towards the teacher and smiled. He stood there for approximately ten seconds and was then helped to put on a smock by the teacher-assistant. He proceeded to paint. When asked what he was painting, the response was 'Colours'. When asked how he knew which brush went into which pot, he replied: 'Red is red, blue is blue, yellow is yellow.'

During the three minutes H carried out approximately ten different actions. The actions included sorting and classifying toys, role-appropriate train-riding, and showing a particular awareness of his teacher and an ability to answer questions. His looking towards the teacher appeared as a point of stability and reassurance; the teacher did not have to return the gaze – she just had to be there. H's actions certainly displayed cognitive and social qualities as well as an affective display (smile) towards the class teacher.

The second observation is of a 4-year-old female in the same classroom and at nearly the same time as the observation of H.

> As observation begins, C is sticking shapes on to a felt board; it appears as if she is making a design. She looks around at the other children in her immediate vicinity who are making screaming noises and continues sticking on shapes. C leaves the design and proceeds to the Wendy House. She enters, looks around inside the house, rocks a cradle and then leaves (all without saying anything). She sits on a large toy tractor and looks towards the climbing frame (from where noise is coming). C 'drives' the tractor around the room, dismounts and carries on walking around the room. She looks, again, at the climbing frame (where four others are 'playing') and goes to it. Entering the door at the rear of the frame she attempts to hold the door (which swings) shut and says: 'I won't let anyone in.' Leaving the door, C climbs up to a platform and states: 'I'm lying down, bedtime.' Others take no notice of C. She looks around, notices me and asks 'What are you doing?' twice. As I am about to answer she turns away – the period is finished.

C participated in over half-a-dozen object-oriented activities and appeared to be very aware of individuals close by. Her use of language was distinctive in two ways. (1) Language was used to provide a narrative of some story/stories formed in her mind and acted upon in the 'play' context. The stories had an immediacy which was dictated by, or responded to, in the immediate context of physical objects (as doors, cradles, etc.) and other individuals' actions. The first use of language had a strong individual use, that is, language was used for private descriptive purposes. (2) Language was also a tool of social communication. C became aware of her observer and showed an inquisitiveness about his presence. She was able to communicate her curiosity. A very relevant fact that arose in the observations of both H and C was that any interaction with people (i.e. between and not simply at individuals) was directed towards adults. Language used in the presence of other children was much more narrative in character.

Within the next two years at school, observations showed children's behaviour to change substantially. There were still elements of both individual and social/interactional 'play', but the ratio of more individual to less social/interactional was reversed. S is a 6-year-old boy, who was observed during an indoor playtime. The teacher was on the other side of the room occupied with other children.

All the children (approximately thirty) are in a classroom and the teacher has allowed a 'free play' period which includes drawing, painting, construction and other activities. S and other boys are taking wooden blocks from a corner to a central area where they are constructing a house/fort. There is much talk among them. S appears to answer questions and take part in conversation. One boy notices me and S looks on. S announces: 'That man is an American.' Another boy answers 'I know'. S carries on gathering and transporting blocks and then places them on the wall to increase its height. He then states (to himself) 'I am getting more', picks up more blocks and transports them to the structure. He enters the structure and is told something (inaudible) by a girl. S replies 'I know'. He finds a pistol-shaped block and lies down behind the wall (as if for protection) and, pointing the block at children outside the wall, makes shooting noises. S says 'Shot you'. He gets up and gathers more blocks and is asked something by another boy; he looks at other boys playing by the structure (fighting with their guns). S carries on building, looks for another 'gun', asks a boy 'Can I have (that block)?' and is told 'No'. He then announces to the other boy playing by the structure; 'We got bombs.' They show the 'bombs' to each other and deposit them inside the structure. Another boy knocks down part of the structure. S says 'Look what you've done' and starts to repair it.

The number of separate activities was very high, although there was an underlying unity among the actions – directed around the fantasy and reality of a war game. S showed mechanical competence in the construction (placement of blocks on an ever-heightening wall) of the fort. He was aware of the observer and recalled information concerning the observer learned several hours previously. Language was used by S in five ways: he was able to answer questions put to him and other play members; he was able to make informative pronouncements about people and objects in the immediate vicinity; at times he maintained a narrative of his ongoing actions; language was used to note his fantasy images of guns and bombs; and S used language as a social/regulatory function to announce that destruction of the fort was not acceptable (although he took it upon himself to repair the structure). Language usage was almost entirely directed towards other children; adults had negligible interaction with the child in the observation, and he did not seek adult attention. Aside from development and usage of language, S occupied himself for the full three minutes in multiple activities centred on a single theme in and around the fort.

By contrast to the free play observation of the 6-year-old, the class-time observation of an 8-year-old female showed strongly directive activity – this time in response to the time restriction imposed by the teacher.

Children are all sitting at their individual places working on an assignment from the teacher. T is working on her handwriting (others have been assigned maths and reading). A girl across from T asks what she is doing. T replies by telling and showing her what she has been doing. The other girl replies 'So am I'. A boy leans across the conversation and expands it to a three-way discussion, with the boy telling what he is doing. T looks up towards the teacher, then looks down and says 'Shhh!', which stops the conversation. They all carry on the exercise. The boy starts another conversation with T (too far away to hear accurately). T looks up at the blackboard, touches her face with her fingers and carries on writing.

One is immediately struck with two aspects of behaviour in the observation of T. First, she was able to get on with assigned work; that is, she understood her responsibility to fulfil the assignment with a minimum of fuss and distraction. Secondly, she was very much aware of the social responsibilities of the classroom; that is, to be quiet (and work). The social responsibility appeared to be 'internalised'. T did not need to be told to be quiet. She maintained legitimacy by referring to (looking directly at, or at the board assignments of) the teacher. The sheer amount of conversation characteristic of the younger children was nonexistent. In place of conversation was assigned classwork. There were no descriptions of fantasy, but verbal communication was extremely well developed. In a short space of time the children were able to compare their assigned exercises and their speed towards completion. The above children were more focused, communicative and controlled by the time that they had reached 8 years of age, after four years in classrooms.

In a purely descriptive way, four children (aged 4, 4, 6 and 8 years) and some of their actions and interactions in primary school classrooms have been noted. While they have been shown to be 'doing' quite different activities, four issues of importance arise. (1) Are the brief activities that have been noted characteristic of the behaviour of these individual children and also of children of each approximate age-group?; (2) While these children's activities may appear quite different, are there basic similarities in what they are doing? (3) How does their stage of development mediate the actual activities that the children are doing and are capable of doing. (4) Given that the descriptions are examples of child behaviour and development, the environment and personnel of the school must be taken into account in that they provide and define the context of adaptation for the child. The first issue seeks information on individual ability, individual differences and more or less describes what a classroom teacher has to cope with on a day-to-day basis (as confirmed in numerous textbooks on educational psychology). The second issue explores the general development of children in perceptual, intellectual and social senses. Why are reception classrooms structured with so much apparatus? Does a child play by him/herself? When a question is asked, is an answer expected? To whom are questions directed (teacher, children, specialist)? What insight does the literature/reality of development provide for understanding children? The third issue is concerned with development and the dynamics that promote and enhance develop- ment in the primary classroom, and may be termed a developmental social psychology of the primary school. The fourth issue is closely tied to the third in its provision of context. Children's introduction to school is often seen as a growing familiarity with the teacher and classroom. Roles and styles of interaction are quickly initiated in the school. These interactions, coupled with the child's developing abili- ties to adapt, shape the child's developing knowledge of the social world. The interactions and adaptation are the subject of this study.

Development, as it has been used thus far, is a catch-all term. The developmental responsibilities of the primary school make it unique as an educational institution. Embodied in its philosophy and practicality are the advancement of the child's intellectual development and the acquisition of social skills and development. All further educational settings (secondary schools, polytechnics, universities, etc.) only pro- vide for intellectual advancement and, perhaps, pastoral care; the development of social skills is assumed to have reached a sufficiently advanced state for entry.

Is it possible to delineate between social and intellectual develop- ment? In the four descriptions above the activities and dynamics of the actors are not drastically different. The children use objects (toys, paints, pencils, counters, etc.) and physically manipulate them. They express thoughts and ideas (statements, questions, writing, painting) and interact with others (by copying similar activities, seeking atten- tion from teacher or classmates, telling experiences to those around, playing games). While the younger child does appear to be engaging in similar activities we might say that older children are more sophisti- cated in their activities (in both range and competence) and have *developed*. Development, then, includes the ability to think and reason, use numbers, manual and physical dexterity, knowledge of games and the rules by which they are played, language used for description of feelings and events, language used for communication to others (teacher and children), creative expression and more. A salient factor in development is that one cannot separate particular perceptual, intellectual and social characteristics. The characteristics develop simultaneously. Development is a product of the child's interaction with the environment; and this environment, especially in the school, is both object- and socially oriented. The child develops by entry into a world full of things and people, a world that helps the child to grow from a self-enclosed being, dependent on parents and care-taker, into a personality and actor.

The role of the primary school is to prepare the child for further education and entry into society in the fullest social sense. Recalling our own memories of early schooldays (of teachers, classrooms, headmasters' books and papers) and reflecting on today's schools – perhaps the buildings, subjects taught and some teaching methods have changed, but the role and function of the primary school have remained the same. Exploration of the preparing role leads in two directions. First, to be taken up later, there is the question of how and why the child is prepared for coming to school: what insight does early social development (mainly dominated by events within the family home) provide for the child's entry into the school?[1] The second direction actually looks into the dynamics of the school (and will be discussed more fully in the third chapter). The dynamics of the primary school appear similar to the list of development characteristics. The primary school is often noted as a main agent in the intellectual development and socialisation of the child. Intellectual development can be described as the amount and type of learning that the child has achieved by the end of his/her primary school years: the ability to read, write, use and apply mathematics, knowledge of elementary science, history, geography, and so on, are all catered for by specific curriculum design. On the other hand, intellectual development may be described from the child's view as a series of stages; the amount and type of thought are mediated by the experiences (interactions) of the child and the increasing ability to abstract and understand the ongoing world. School experiences invariably have a social basis (a continuation from the home). The school introduces the child to teachers and other children (and other personnel). Social/school experiences appear to develop in a similar pattern to intellectual stages. But social develop-ment emphasises the reliance on emotional/affective attachment be-tween the child and *significant others*, a point made explicitly by the Plowden Commission (1967). General social development is described in Chapter 3. The interaction of the social, intellectual and affective aspects of development forms the basis for the later study.

This volume does not actively discuss or debate how the child develops intellectually. There are numerous books and reviews which concern themselves with interpretations of development from which characterisations of abilities and experiences may be drawn. Perhaps the least contentious stand to take is to state that as children grow older and have more experiences they become more able to use advanced and abstract thought. Advancements in the intellect are often characterised by 'stage': a concept used to denote differing and progressive organisation of thought and ability to adapt new information. The stages of intellectual development are best described by Piaget and Inhelder (1969). Through intense observations and interviewing, they described four stages and means (schemes) by which information is adapted. (*a*) The *sensori-motor* stage is dominated by perceptual development, culminating in the realisation of object permanence and ability to use words and symbols; advancement of thought is dominated by the child's actions and the range of possible 'things to do' in the surrounding environment. The child repeats actions over and again, gradually taking in and accommodating new and stimulating events. (*b*) In the *pre-operational* stage the child is beginning to understand causation but is still dominated by activities; hence play with sand, water, words, and so on. The child is not able to reflect upon actual reasons why something has happened. Events 'happen' and do not lead to any particular insight about similar events. The child must 'do' (either physically or mentally) in order to understand; thought is dominated by the process and not the logic of doing. (*c*) During the *concrete operations* stage, where realisation of cause takes place simultaneously with the action, the child is able to understand why and how – thought processes take place within the child's mind. The child can 'reverse' and 'conserve' and perform other logical-mathematical operations. But the child is still caught in the here-and-now, able to understand what can be seen in reality, but unable to understand the theoretical or principled basis for events. (*d*) In the *formal operations* stage the child has the ability to abstract, hypothesise and deduce and is no longer tied to physical manipulation of objects. Principle and theory can dominate understanding; the child is no longer limited to the here-and-now.

The stages of intellectual development show the child actively to construct an understanding of the surrounding environment. Piaget's theory of stage development stressed that: (1) each stage is different from the others; (2) each stage sets the basis for the stage that follows; (3) the stages are passed through by everyone in the sequence noted; (4) the stages form a hierarchy; (5) once the individual has progressed to a further stage all previous stages remain usable within the individual's cognitive 'repertoire';[2] (6) underlying the child's development and organisation of thought is the process of adaptation, incorporating the processes of assimilation (the taking in or acknowledging of new information) and accommodation (the development of previous knowledge to understand and make use of newly assimilated information); and (7) the process of adaptation is constrained by the child's environment (that is, the amount and type of stimulation and restriction/freedom will be represented in the child's thought). There have been several researchers who have challenged the make-up and precise progression of the stages described by Piaget (for example, studies qualifying the development of identity/equivalence conducted by Bryant, 1974, Donaldson, 1978, and others). The challengers do show earlier existence of aspects of some stages than previously thought, but do not seriously affect the progression characteristic of the theory.

Simultaneous with intellectual development, Piaget (1959) also described stages of social development. Socially the child moves from an undifferentiated autistic stage (where the child appears unaware of him/herself, objects and other people) to an *ego-centric* stage (where the child's thought is dominated by the self). The child is able to adapt to sensory and perceptual events and to differentiate him/herself from objects. But the child does not perceive that there are different ways of viewing an object or that other people have wants, desires, or rules different from his/her own. A *socialised* stage is reached (through play, communication, games with rules) when the child realises that others have their individual thoughts, wants and desires that may be different from the child's. The socialised stage sets a background for moral, friendship, political and other social developments.

Intellectual and social development do take place at the same time. The age-span of children in primary schools, from 4½ to 11 years, covers development from pre-operations to the start of formal operations and the advancement from ego-centric to social stages. In view of active development by the child, the school must be aware of its responsibilities in both intellectual and social senses. While promoting advancement of thought and reasoning, the school also promotes the friendships, morals and political orientation of the child. The child is seen, especially in the more progressive and open primary schools, as capable and competent. The child adapts to the environment of the school and in doing so assimilates or takes in new information and makes use of, or accommodates, this information into his/her mental structure (understanding). To thereby assemble an adequate understanding of the developing social world of the school we must take into account the general environment of the school, the actions and interactions that the child has with people and objects, the understanding that the child has of these actions and the background of social development that the child brings to school from home. The first three aspects noted above will, hopefully, be illuminated throughout the next chapters; from descriptions of actual school behaviours a theory of development and schooling will be generated. The home background will be briefly reviewed here to set the stage for school introduction.

HOME BACKGROUND

The child's readiness for introduction to the school is based upon early development in the home and its immediate surroundings.[3] Perceptual, intellectual and social characteristics of development will here be described in part; it should be remembered that they take place simultaneously. The following few pages focus on the first year of life as an example of the integrated development of the child. Examples of the early capacities of the child are cited and expanded into abilities through interaction with people and objects.

The child is born with a capacity to display quite complex behaviours and dispositions. The neonate, or newborn infant, demonstrates a wide range of reflexes: touching the palm of the hand causes the fingers to clench into a grasp (palmar); touching the bottom of the foot causes the toes to curl over (plantar); touching the side of the face brings the head to turn in the direction of the touch and sucking reflex (rooting); the child will pull his/her head away and close its eyes if an object is seen coming directly at it; the child can cry and make various noises; the neonate also shows balance; and, if supported with feet touching a flat surface and gently leaning forward, walking abilities. There are many other reflexes the neonate displays, but the above are sufficient to show that behaviours exist which may be attributed to a phylogenetic, biological pre-adaptation to life.[4] The reflexes also show that the neonate is born with a developed sensory system. According to Bower (1977), the neonate has six senses at birth: taste, smell, hearing, sight, touch and propriocentration (an awareness of physical position and movement of different parts of the body, progressing from gross head and limb movement to more refined muscular abilities). The child is also capable of 'learning' in operant and classical senses (Millar, 1974). Using these senses, initially from reflex at birth, the child generates a more refined perceptual understanding of the self and surrounding environment. The reflexes gradually disappear after the first month of life. Behaviours such as grasping, watching and movement reappear, but are now closely controlled and further developed by the child. The reflexes show active sensory and learning qualities. They also serve as a means of communication between infant and caretaker, a capacity from birth to be social.

By centring on just two of the senses (sight and sound), early development can be shown to have a strong social character. From birth the ears and eyes appear well developed. In actuality the neonate is born with a partially functioning system of sight. The retina (light-sensitive surface at the back of the eye) is fairly well developed, but the centre of the retina (macula) is only partially developed. The optic nerves are in existence but the protective coating (myelin sheath) has not been completed. The infant can control the amount of light entering the eye by dilating and constricting the pupil. The infant appears to judge distance (through binocular parallax, motion parallax and optical expansion, see Bower, 1974, for a full discussion). At birth the neonate can focus on objects approximately 8 inches from the face for maximum clarity. By 4 months the ability to control the lens (for image clarity) is similar to an adult's (Haynes *et al.*, 1965). Studies by Fantz and his colleagues showed infant viewing preference by offering the child a choice of two images to look at, and recording the amount of time spent focused on one or the other choice. In their research Fantz *et al.* (1962) concluded that the neonate could perceive form and pattern. There was a preference for complex as opposed to simple stimuli. Fantz (1961) further showed that from one week after birth the child preferred to view images of the human face rather than any other image (even if the features of the face were scrambled). When Wilcox (1969) compared realistic to scrambled faces he found no particular preference by children between 4 and 16 weeks, but after 4 months a photograph of a female face was preferred to a realistic facial drawing.

The neonate has the ability to hear stereophonically (through both ears) and to see. Stereophonic hearing means that a single sound from a source may reach each of the child's ears at a slightly different time, and hence provide different patterns of sound and intensity. Each discrepancy produces cues for the individual which help to distinguish the source, location and type of sound. The infant's ability to discriminate and locate sounds (coming from objects) in darkness has been demonstrated in early infancy (Bower and Wishart, 1973) for objects straight ahead of the child. The ability to locate was reduced if the sound source was off to one side or the other; but if the child was able to see an object the ability to locate and grasp for it was greatly increased. Stepping into the social world of the infant, Aronson and Rosenbloom (1971) placed 3-week-old babies in a sound-proof room where they could see their mothers (straight ahead of them), through a glass screen. The mother was asked to speak to the child and the voice was transmitted stereophonically to loudspeakers in separate corners in the front of the room. If the speakers were adjusted so that the voice came from one side rather than straight ahead the child became very disturbed. Doing the same experiment with older children, Aronson and Dunfield (1972) found infants became distressed but also showed a 'double orientation' of looking at the mother while turning their heads to centre on the source of the sound. In both of Aronson's studies some cognitive co-ordination or expectation by the infant was demonstrated by presenting stimuli counter to that knowledge. Many other experiments have been conducted exploring the generation of auditory and visual capacities of the young child (for reviews see Bower, 1974, and McGurk, 1974). I have drawn upon this information only to demonstrate that from birth the infant is aware of his/her environment through sensory capacities and maintains the ability to form a cognitive understanding or representation. Just how all senses combine in development is a subject still open for researchers.

From both practical and experimental experience one can see the evolution of these behaviours towards a preference for nearness to a particular parent or caretaker by approximately 6 months. With increasing mental capacities the child becomes aware of objects and people in the surrounding environment. Parents and caretakers, for their part, provide stimulating experience for the child beyond sight and sound. These adults pick up, cuddle, feed and change the baby, to name a few stimuli. They are also novel experiences in themselves and introduce the child to further new experiences. Children's awareness and knowledge of these adults precede the Piagetian stage of object permanence. It was about this discrepancy that Piaget and Inhelder hypothesised when they stated that intellectual and social development take place in parallel. To explain further, the child first develops in a sensori-motor stage, where thought is dominated by actions and sensory (non-verbal) understanding. The child's knowledge expands from familiar (acted upon) objects to symbolic representation. Physically, the parent or caretaker is a major element in this development. This adult is probably the most familiar, highly interactive and stimulating object for the child. And the child can provide no greater acknowledgement than by perceiving and remembering this person among the first of all objects that are remembered and recognised. The actual dynamics of this interaction sensori-motor development will be taken up in Chapter 2.

I shall only extend the subject here to note that Schaffer (1971) and others have introduced the subject of social perception as a basis of child–adult interaction (signalling, responsiveness, sensitivity) through which the child becomes familiar with the adult and eventually forms a bond[5] of trust or dependence. The interaction and resulting bond are used by many social scientists as the preliminary basis for theories of socialisation. At this point one could introduce theoretical arguments concerning the nature of rule-learning, social meanings, and so on, from reinforcement, identification and other views of development; but they would be superfluous to this review based upon biological, social and cognitive pre-adaptations of the child. A further view of social development from birth has been presented by Dubin and Dubin (1963), who term the first years of the child's life the 'authority inception period', whereby the child realises a dependent relationship towards parents. Through the interaction process the child progresses from physical and emotional dependence (feeding, comfort, etc., from parents), to bowel and bladder control, to a social-rule-bound and convention-oriented understanding of relations. The child has learnt the rudiments of acting and interacting as a social being. Stayton, Hogan and Ainsworth (1971) provide greater insight with their finding that 'a disposition toward obedience emerges in a responsive, accommodating social environment without extensive training, discipline, or other massive attempts to shape the infant's course of development (p. 1065)' in children less than 1 year old. The finding that obedience occurs so early in childhood and that it is strongly linked to bonding illuminates the fact that early social development has a basis in an authority relationship between caretaker and child. The authority relationship is structured through early adaptation in the upbringing context, and sets a basis for further authority, moral and social developments (to be discussed in Chapter 2).

The child's social pre-adaptiveness is usually seen as centring on parent or caretaker. Through the strength of this bond the child is introduced into a wider social world of other adults, peers and the school. Traumas in the upbringing situation may alter the strength of the bond and ease of entry into the further social world, but do not destroy its existence. Similarly, other home or upbringing variables such as birth order, number of siblings, or social class will have varying effects on ease of entry to the social world, but will not negate the existence of the child–parent (caretaker) relationship. We may term, for future reference, the recognition of the existence of such a relationship as a cognitive understanding. The merits, strength and general applicability of the relationship is mediated through affective development. For, while we may note the existence of bonding, obedience, and so on, we must place these findings in the context of developing mental abilities, social relations, stimulation and the trust and security which the child seeks in the formation of close relationships.

NOTES: CHAPTER 1

1 In research into development one can take one of two approaches: via abnormal/ pathological situations, or via normal development. Until the last decade the social sciences had a tendency to use the former. With the vast increase of research into intellectual and social development, especially that carried out by Piaget and his colleagues, we are able to piece together a picture of the developing child based upon normal cognitive growth processes. This book will mainly expand on the second approach, but in such a way that the reader may be able to draw insights about possible breakdowns of this normal development.

2 Hence one may find a teacher explaining a concept to pupils in formal operational (abstract) terms. If a pupil is unable to understand the concept the teacher will ask him/her to think back to a similar, but personal, incident, thereby using a concrete operation. Or if a mathematical problem is unsolvable on paper the teacher may ask a child to use Cuisinaire rods or Necar cubes.

3   Again as in note 1, we may describe early development as normal or non-normal. Normal development would assume a home environment with a two-parent family. Non-normal early development may take place in an orphanage or some other institution, or within a family that is breaking up or has broken up. The basic cognitive (social and intellectual) processes of the child will remain the same in both situations, although emotional upheaval may slow the rate of advance. This book will expand upon a normative model while acknowledging the existence of other models.

4   These reflexes have been useful in the evolutionary past and many are necessary still to maintain the child's life and development. For example, the cluster of crying, clinging and sucking conspire to evolve a system of communication between child and caretaker that provides for feeding, relief of discomfort and general care.

5   The 'bond' relationship, again, is referred to in a Western, single-family home. Bonding is not limited to the relationship between the child and members of his/her family; rather what is stressed is the relationship that the child has with a person or persons and the stimulations that they provide for the child. Bonding can hypothetically take place in communal (kibbutz, communist country, or child institution) environments as well as in the family home.

Chapter 2

Social and Moral Development

In Chapter 1 I gave examples of the parallel developments in the child's early and social life. The present chapter is set to describe social development in greater detail. Instead of presenting a unified (cf. Erikson, 1972) view of development, or a maturational notation (Gesell and Ilg, 1965) of child reactions and capabilities, instances of play, language as communication and moral development will be used to exemplify the years of early and middle childhood. Incidents are chosen to present a structural basis for the book's developmental perspective. Organisational points on the role of schemes and their relation to actions, and the movement from an egocentric to sociocentric understanding, will be drawn from the literature. Combining details from the above examples with the child's upbringing context (home, caretakers, etc.), a pattern of social authority presentation and understanding will be framed (for future discussion) and discussed in relation to social and moral developments. The chapter will conclude by organising the literature reviewed into a more coherent view of development, drawing upon individuals in the child's life (who have been termed agents of socialisation) and schemes by which the child adapts to the environment; in other words, I shall present a crude social-psychological theory of socialisation.

PLAY

Observation of an infant's social and intellectual interactions can be most time-consuming and exacting, yet absorbing and interesting. Both parent and researcher easily get caught up in game-like interactions with the child. As described in Chapter 1, the child's senses and reflexes form a basis for interaction with caretaker from birth. The child's ability to regulate the use of the senses (by closing the eyes, opening the eyes wide, turning the head away, making sounds) in response to stimulation by the caretaker approximates a give-and-take or taking-turn sequence reminiscent of games and conversation. The quality of interaction is also regulated by the expression on the baby's face. Stern (1977) has noted that facial expressions are organised by the child from about 6 weeks of age, and are: surprise, frown, concern, sympathy and a neutral expression. These facial expressions are quickly tied to actual bodily states (of pleasure, need, displeasure, etc.). These expressions serve as *reciprocal* signals for communication and concern generated between the child and people around it. Stern has noted the integration of the infant's sensory and communicative development with the human environment, expanding previous researchers' views of the young infant from a purely sensory orientation to one of *sensory-affective* units.

Visual and vocal contact between the child and those around it prepare for early recognition of caretaker (as discussed in Chapter 1). Once recognition is achieved, a basis for early games with rules is set. Bruner and Sherwood (1976) cite the game 'Peekaboo' as one of the 'most universal forms of play between adults and infants'. The rules noted by Bruner and Sherwood were generated in a sequence that started with a contact between mother and infant, the former looming or appearing in front of the child. Having established a contact, the mother quickly disappeared from sight and then reappeared and visual/re-established contact. Once this convention was established the mother and sometimes the infant were able to vary timing, masking (putting hands in front of face, objects in front of face, around corner, etc.) and vocalisations. After contact and variations were established the initiator of the game varied from mother to infant, acknowledging that the child's newly acquired skills in movement (rolling over, crawling) could provide new formats for the game as well as variations introduced by the mother. 'An old pattern seems, then, to provide a framework for the pleasurable expression of new behaviour and allows the new behaviour to be quickly incorporated into a highly skilled, rule-governed pattern' (p. 284). Depending on the mastery of skills (remembering, locating, etc.) that the child has acquired, further variations of the game develop. Greenfield (1970) found the game was played by 12-week-old infants and their mothers; the younger infants would play only if they could see their mother as well as hear her. The necessity for voice contact declined with age. Two basic elements of the child's social development can be drawn from this example of early play: (1) play requires specific skill mastery by the child – here the skills of memory and recognition were drawn upon; (2) there is a necessary social relationship that promotes the play and generates sequences in the behaviour and, hence, rules for the organisation of these behaviours. The quality and development of peekaboo will vary with the degree of sensitivity of caretaker to infant and vice versa, emphasising the importance of an affective/emotional relationship.

It is very difficult to state what play is exactly. As Garvey (1977) has noted, a child told to 'go out and play' will often question the term: 'What do you mean, play?' It is more easily understood if the child is directed to 'build a sand castle' or 'ride your bike'. Instead of defining play, Garvey lists characteristics which incorporate the mastery and social qualifications described in peekaboo.

(1) Play is pleasurable and enjoyable.
(2) Play has no extrinsic goals.
(3) Play is spontaneous and voluntary.
(4) Play involves some active engagement on the part of the player.
(5) Play has certain systematic relations to what is not play. (p. 10)

The first four points of the list are self-explanatory. The fifth point is very extensive. Play may be linked to creativity, problem-solving, language-learning, acknowledgement of social roles and more. As the reader may all too easily see, the fifth point includes cognitive, social and affective elements. It is difficult to cite examples of childhood play that can adequately differentiate between mastery and social skills which underlie the elements.

Play as Mastery
Mastery may be noted as the ability (skills) with which a child uses tools and other objects. Having advanced to a sufficient state of intellectual and physical maturity to acknowledge object permanence, the child is able to explore use of objects as tools. Outside the realm of child development, Lawick-Goodall (1976) has described early tool usage in chimpanzees. She observed a community of chimpanzees in their natural environment. One of the behaviours that Lawick-Goodall frequently observed was adults 'fishing' for termites by inserting sticks with the bark stripped off into entrance passage (holes) of termite hills. Termites bit on the tools. The chimpanzees withdrew the sticks and licked the termites off. The following was observed in 'learning' to use this *tool*. From about 9 months, infants observed their mothers at the task. Between 1 and 2 years the infants started picking up grasses and twigs and 'stripping' them – as if preparing the tool. At 2 years they gripped twigs and attempted to jab at the surface of the hill. Between 2 and 4 years inappropriate materials and clumsy techniques were discarded and length of time practising the inserting movement increased. By 4 years most chimpanzees showed an adult technique. The infant chimpanzee, not unlike the child trying to build a tower of wooden blocks or kick a ball between two upright sticks, must master elementary movement and thought techniques. In so doing, they gain *competence* in using tools. Similarly, the peekaboo game demonstrates children's mastery at an earlier age. Between 4 and 6 months of age the child shows an ability to blink, turn his/her head away, put hands in front of eyes – and other variations to contact and break contact with caretaker. The movements may appear infantile and insignificant. But they allow the infant to initiate, maintain and adapt social contacts.

Further, the game may result in the recognition of person permanence and elementary physical laws.

Social Play/Competence
The child's play activities provide an arena for development of competence. I have already shown examples of mastery, but social aspects must now be expanded within the two contexts of social skill and the social environment. It is almost impossible to unravel the skill from the environmental elements. The peekaboo game is a preliminary example in which a social convention is demonstrated – that of give-and-take, action–response, similar to a conversation. While words and sounds are not necessarily included, the action (intention)–response sequence does exemplify the behavioural acts of a *conversation*. Trevarthen (1975) has explored early attempts at conversation in the first few weeks of life. He records specific patterns of movement made by infants in response to the presence and communications of their mothers. Infants appeared to recline or strain forward in co-ordination with their mother's speaking or remaining silent. The infants actually showed and made movements in sequence to maintain the conversation. Phrasing of maternal speech allowed the child some form of response before the conversation could continue. In interacting with parent or caretaker the infant is exposed to a new range of sounds, expressions and behaviours which are quickly assimilated. The caretaker relationship provides stimulation for the child. During sensorimotor development much research has centred on the child–adult interaction as a basis for cognitive growth; perhaps Stern's description of the relationship in sensory-affective units best defines the relationship and types of interaction.

Competence is a broad concept which relates to 'manipulation, locomotion, language, the building of cognitive maps and skilled actions and the growth of effective behaviour in relation to other people' (White, 1960, p. 137). Nardine draws further upon emotional and motivational issues in his definition of competence as the 'individual's ability to take the initiative and act upon his environment' (1971, p. 336). For competent acts to take place, the individual requires knowledge (mastery) and self-confidence. Competence, then, is gained in a free and experimental situation that contains objects and people; where the child may play in an uninhibited manner. Competence is not the word used by children to explain their activities. It is defined by the individual child in his/her intellectual and social circumstances – just ask a child what she/he is doing and how.

While noting the theoretical importance of social play, I have avoided describing its practical nature. What are the events that actually happen? Very early instances of social play have already been described in the peekaboo sequence. Numerous other activities between infant and caretaker may also be noted for their reciprocal nature, whether initiated by the child or the adult. The ability to make sounds – from initial babbling to carefully shaped words – is important, both for play quality and for later *communication* using language. Sounds made by the child may be spontaneous and bring some sign of recognition or pleasure by caretaker. Imitation of sounds and noises helps to extend the *vocabulary* of the child and link these noises to objects and people. The older and more mobile child will have a greater number of 'things' to see and imitate. With the ability to use language and words as symbols, the child can fantasise and project him/herself into new and experimental situations. Children often link the sound of the object that they are playing with to the actual situation; hence one often sees the 3-year-old boy on a small cart or trolley and hears sounds reminiscent of a speedway, fire engine, or police car.

Fantasy at this age (2–5 years) is often strongly linked to sex stereotypes. Fantasy allows the child to use symbols to act out and practise unobtainable scenes which promote intellectual, social and emotional development (see Vygotsky, 1967, for further discussion). An early example of fantasy is a child using a broomstick for a horse. Children in playgroups and pre-school nurseries often re-enact family situations. Favourite toys (dolls, action men, cars) are brought to the groups by the children and used to allow the children to act as if they were adults of their own sex. Children of creche age are aware of sex differences (boys, girls) and can point out differences on sex-typed dolls (Thompson, 1975). Play in the Wendy House 'allows' girls to put dolls in bed, prepare tea and generally tidy up. Boys come into the house for tea, but note that they have to go out to 'work'. Generally boys are the ones who get into the 'car' and drive away. From interviews concerning knowledge of mothers and fathers with children as young as 4½ years, Kutnick (1974) has demonstrated the impact of the home in the development of sex stereotypes and the background to the above roles. When asked about mummies and daddies, virtually all of the children said that 'mummies do the cooking and buy the food'. Mummies are also the people who 'tell you to straighten up the room' or 'go and get something from the shop'. Daddies, on the other hand, 'fix things', 'wash the car' and 'go out to work'. It was surprising to find such strong stereotypes, especially when so many mothers in the area worked. It appeared that basic relationships in the home were not challenged even when the 'work' relationship was. Children's knowledge of their parents was based upon their mothers' and fathers' actual behaviours in the home.

An interesting and necessary aside focuses attention on a child's developing knowledge in relation to that child's actual behaviour. Any parent, child worker, or researcher will have much observational experience of a child repeating behaviours over and again. Whether it is the sound of a police siren or the careful placement of plastic cups and saucers on a table, the behaviours are repeated until the child has a working knowledge of the behaviour and its meaning. The movement from behaviour to knowledge can be described in terms of assimilation and accommodation, in a scheme similar to pre-operational development. A confounding, but vitally important, conclusion to draw from these discussions is that children are 'free' to behave in certain ways (which are linked to knowledge), but the behaviours available to the child are often limited by the models of behaviour to which the child has access. The child's behaviours are bound to a large extent by the context of parents' behaviour. To take this point a stage further, the reader may see the child's sex stereotypical behaviour and knowledge as an expression of those individuals (usually parents) with whom the child interacts.

Further, behavioural differences between boys and girls have been described and noted in Blurton Jones's (1976) study of rough-and-tumble play among 3- to 5-year-olds. The study used the ethological method of writing down behaviours as they occurred and then reviewing notes for *patterns of action* repeated by the children. Quite different from rough-and-tumble play, Blurton Jones first noted *agonistic* behaviour taking place between many of the children – displayed most often when one child wanted and took a toy or item that another was playing with. The attacking child usually fixated on the item and threatened a blow (described in detail by Blurton Jones) with a frowning expression on his/her face. The robbed child gave a scream (the type of scream depended on whether he/she was hit or not) and assumed either an attacking or a defensive position. Verbal behaviour was not a part of this sequence. More often, though, rough-and-tumble would be displayed in the nursery play situation. Seven movements have been described by Blurton Jones in rough-and-tumble play: running, chasing and fleeing, wrestling, jumping up and down with both feet together, beating at each other with an open hand without actually hitting, beating at each other with an item without actually hitting, and laughing. Children always had a smile expression during rough-and-tumble play, which differentiated it from agonistic behaviour. This play is of interest to ethologists as a valid description of child behaviour and maintains similarity to other primates and their childhood behaviour. Rough-and-tumble play often looks like hostile agonistic behaviour to adults and can easily become so. The play requires interaction between at least two children, with sequences (almost conversational) of behaviour often started by one child and repeated by another. Boys, according to Blurton Jones, participate in this play to a greater extent than girls; but this may only be reflective of upbringing practices in the home. Activities in rough-and-tumble do allow children to practise further social interactions, property and dominance relationships in the relative calm of the play situation.

Games and Rules

The conversational quality of play between children is reminiscent of, and may be seen to precede, actual play with rules – more properly known as games. Piaget (1965) has provided very insightful examples of rules in the Genevan game of marbles, and the useful distinction between the behavioural practice of rules and the child's conscious knowledge of them. (Marbles is not a single game, and even one type of game, e.g. shooting a marble to knock others out of a square, has many variations between where it is played, by whom it is played and when it is played.) Piaget asked various children to play a square game and refresh his memory on how it was played. His observation of play showed four stages of the practice of rules. First, *motor and individual character* in which the child handled the marbles in the way he/she wished, and spoke of motor rules (basically of the physical movement). Secondly, *ego-centric* following of rules in which the child was aware of codified rules, but applied them only to him/herself – hence although a few children would play the game at the same time, they each 'imitated' the rules that they knew and more than one child would win the same competitive match in his/her own right. Thirdly, *incipient co-operation* in which individual children tried to win and in so doing questioned the control of rules, but ideas concerning the origin of rules were vague. And fourthly, *codification of rules* in which all details of the procedure were agreed, fixed and known by all players; this stage was not observed until 11–12 years of age. The consciousness of rules followed a similar progression, but in three progressive stages. At the first stage rules were purely motor and interesting examples; the rules were not seen as 'coercive' in any way. In the second stage (covering a span of ego-centric and co-operative practice stages noted above) the child regarded rules as sacred, coming from adults, and any alteration was wrong. Rules used by others, especially respected others, were copied and applied to the best of the child's ability. A rule was accepted as law only with mutual consent in the third stage; children could alter rules if everyone playing was willing to agree. Sacredness of rules was broken down to allow co-operative control.

A fundamental insight into patterns or schemes of social development is repeated in Piaget's research on moral judgement. In observing the developmental sequence of playing the game and knowledge of the rules, one finds conscious knowledge lagging behind the physical use of rules. In other words, patterns of behaviour in play preceded children's verbal knowledge of what and why they were doing it. This developmental trend may best exemplify Piaget's (1962) assertion that play is only an act of assimilation; it is up to the child to come to an understanding of the behaviour and accommodate his/her mental structures. Numerous examples of children's behaviour developing are found in everyday activities, such as water-play (leading to conservation), attempting to fit variously shaped objects into holes (hopefully of the appropriate size), the movement of random painting and drawing strokes into the recognisable depiction of an object, and the playing of certain characters – leading very often to identification with that character.

Insight drawn from the use of co-operation provides an important example here: the behavioural stage of incipient co-operation was observed in 7- to 8-year-olds and occurred during the two or three years before the conscious realisation of mutual consent. The pattern of behaviour preceding awareness is similar to the intellectual pre-operative stage of development (described in Chapter 1). The realisation of mutual consent (co-operation) came through the clash of incomplete understanding of rules and inevitable conflicts that arose from individual children's interpretation of rules, according to Piaget. The actions in conflict (argument, discussion, etc.) facilitated the evolution from an ego-centric to a social perspective. Once the children were able to understand the common basis of rules, they were able to apply the rules concretely in further games; Piaget noted that many of the boys he observed 'seem to take a particular pleasure in anticipating all possible cases and in codifying them'.

It is difficult to provide a fair summary of Piaget's research on games and rules, but three themes vital to an understanding of social development should be noted. First, the child progressed from a non-knowledge of rules to an ego-centric application to a socialised application. Secondly, rules were initially perceived as outside the control of children and dominated by adults. Through social interaction, mutual consent and control were realised – a co-operation among equals. Thirdly, there appeared a clear parallel of schemes of social development with those of intellectual development. A fourth theme may be deduced from the above three and previous examples. It acknowledges that all behaviour (and development) takes place within a context. The context is bound by the models of behaviour and the type of objects, and so on, found in the child's environment. Denzin (1977) interestingly cites several examples of the limit imposed by the context on the child's play and political relations by parents and schools. The following section will look more closely into the transition from ego-centric to social perspectives by exploring the developing use of language in the age-grouping between 4 and 11 years.

LANGUAGE

Observing the play of a nursery-aged child provides many examples of the varied language and communicative possibilities that he/she has at hand. Beyond the initial labelling of gross overt physical actions as behaviour, the reader must extend the definition of behaviour to include verbal utterances. Sounds and words become and are indicative of object permanence and symbolic thought. Verbal utterances are similar in development to the more overt physical behaviour.

The use of sounds and words integrates necessary social and intellectual qualities for development. The boy in Chapter 1 who pushed himself around on a toy train calling out 'Choo, choo, train coming' seemed to be making this communication solely for his own and the train's benefit. His painting dictated the type and quality of his conversation; he was painting 'colours'. The words he spoke were descriptive of the actions he was doing or had done. His communications were concerned with his present behaviour. Further, his social communications were mainly adult-oriented: whether he just looked across the classroom to see the teacher and then carried on an activity, said something to the teacher (whether on the other side of the room or not), or just waited for some adult recognition.

The actions of the 6-year-old boy were quite different. The observed actions took place during an indoor playtime. He displayed various abilities. He made symbolic use of an oddly shaped piece of wood as a gun. He, and others, combined in their symbolic conceptualisation of a line of plastic blocks as a fort. He used various rules/responsibilities of fort behaviour (construction, destruction, reconstruction). He also showed behaviours which were similar to and co-operative with other children playing around the fort. He made statements to his playmates concerning the actions in progress. Questions were asked about the availability of other toys. He made a statement to another child: 'That man is an American.' The second child responded 'I know' – a simple but completed conversation. He demonstrated linguistic ability, role-appropriate behaviours and social/co-operative actions among peers. Children of this age-group responded willingly to teacher direction. In the group situation it had become almost habit to raise one's hand when the child wished to ask a question or respond to the teacher. A dual-centredness was strongly evident in the description of the 8-year-old girl. She fulfilled the teacher's work requirements but also carried on a two- and three-way conversation with others around her. Children in her class were very willing to comment on and help others in the classroom, often to the dismay of the teacher as the sheer volume of conversation rose and rose. Children were shown to be effective at responding to the teacher's questions. They followed teacher- and self-directed activities. They questioned for clarification. All of the children were able to communicate effectively using words and signs.

A further example of the development of conversation took place within and immediately outside a classroom of 8-year-olds. The conversation was directive in that specific information was being sought. The conversation concerned a classroom incident and the children's responses to their own and their teacher's actions. Speech and thought were well developed. The conversation centred on rules and roles.

D (boy) and S (girl) had been pushing each other's paper off their table. S stood up and told the teacher (Mrs C). S returned and told D that Mrs C wanted to see him. D went to Mrs C and was asked 'What is the matter with you?' D did not reply and is sent into the corridor to finish his work. I went over to S and started a conversation.

Self:	What happened?
S:	Mrs C sent him out.
Self:	Why?
S:	Because he was sliding things around.
Self:	What things?
S:	Books and papers.
Self:	Why was he doing that?
S:	I don't know.
Self:	Did you do anything?
S:	No.
Self:	Didn't you push anything around yourself?
S:	No.
Self:	Why did he do it?
S:	—— (no reply)
Self:	Did you do anything to him? (to note past interactions)
S:	Sometimes I say things.
Self:	What things?
S:	Well, when he looks over at my book I say that he is cheating. He says that he isn't and pushes my books around. So I told Mrs C and she sent him out.
Self:	Why can Mrs C send him out?
S:	Don't know.
Self:	Is it because she is a teacher?
S:	Yes.

The conversation continues with D in the corridor.

Self:	Why are you out here?
D:	Mrs C sent me.
Self:	Why did she send you?
D:	I pushed S's books on to the floor.
Self:	Why did you do that?
D:	She asked me to push them off.
Self:	Why?

D: I was looking at her book.
Self: Her sum book?
D: No, the cover of her English book.
Self: Where was her English book?
D: On top of her sum book.
Self: S said that you were cheating. Do you know what cheating is?
D: Yes, copying someone else's work.
Self: Were you cheating?
D: No.
Self: It must have looked like cheating.
D: Yes, but it wasn't.
Self: Then what happened.
D: S told me to push the book off. Then she went to Mrs C and Mrs C sent me out.
Self: Why did she do that?
D: I don't know.
Self: Why could Mrs C send you out here?
D: I don't know . . . That's the rule, if you've done something you get sent out.
Self: For how long?
D: Until I finish my sums.

I return to S.

Self: D said that you told him to push your book off the desk, did you?
S: No.
Self: Are you sure?
S: ———
Self: D said that he was looking at your English book, but your English book was covering your sums, why was this?
S: So he wouldn't cheat.

I return to D.

Self: S said that she did not ask you to push the book off.
D: I thought she did (and repeats himself).

The two children involved in these conversations obviously had the ability to communicate with one another in verbal and non-verbal senses. Their time in the classroom was strictly bound by roles (of pupils and teachers) and a system of rules and regulations. Transgressions against the rules were punishable. The punishment, though, was determined by the teacher. Respect for rules was, and is, bound up with authority figures. Language allows conversation to take place but it takes place in a social context of roles, rules and obligations.

The examples of conversation and general comments on the context in which they were made (cited above) coincide with the development of language again researched by Piaget (1959). Being one of his earliest works, *Language and Thought* has weathered quite well. Piaget here attempted to explain the background to two major elements in his theory. The first element was that he let 'fact take precedence over theory'. Instead of applying a previously formulated model of development, he observed the functions of language as used for communication between children. Children's earliest words appeared to be of command, calling out for attention. From his observations, Piaget categorised types and functions of speech into the following:

Repetition – an imitation, the child is often not actively conscious of this act.

Monologue – child speaks and describes own acts, usually as the acts are happening.

Dual or Collective Monologue – similar to above but child appears to be talking to an audience, but does not succeed in making the audience listen.

Adapted Information – child adapts to the point of view of the listener by telling something of interest.

Criticism – remarks about behaviour of others from own point of view.

Commands, Requests, Threats – child asserts a definite type of interaction.

Questions

Answers

In observing these functions, Piaget noted that the first three (Repetition, Monologue and Collective Monologue) were dominated by an inability to perceive and make use of another's point of view. Each of the other functions had an audience in mind for the speaker. Piaget labelled these two groupings as *ego-centric* and *socialised* (as earlier used in games and rules). He noted *decentration* as the transitional factor between ego-centric and socialised speech (and also in conservation). Decentration is the ability to shift attention from the child's individual point of view to an awareness of another's point of view. (In conservation decentration is the ability to shift attention from one aspect of an object or situation to another, e.g. from height to height and width when comparing the amount of water poured from one beaker into another.)

The ability to perceive another's point of view or situation is enhanced by the child's role-taking ability (to be discussed later). The transition from ego-centric to socio-centric was not an all-at-once change. Piaget noted that the development towards socio-centrism was proportional. Younger children had a higher proportion of ego-centric speech – hence the appearance of commands at a predominantly ego-centric stage. Older children had a higher proportion of socio-centric speech. Three stages of language development were described in the following pattern: (1) *ego-centric*; (2) *awareness of presence of others*, but assertion of own point of view – children did activities together and often argued for their own ends; (3) *social*, where there was collaboration in thought and argument – questions were asked, responses expected and children were able to make use of each other's information. (Examples of these three stages can be drawn from the opening observations in the book.)

In both *Language and Thought* and *Moral Judgement of the Child* Piaget noted that the role of the peer group is vitally important for social awareness and co-operation. Children interacting with other children of similar age, size, experience, and so on, provide an all-too-vague but necessary foundation for the transition to socio-centrism. Children provide models for each other. They have different and extensive experiences which can be shared with others. In the case of rule development, children must compromise their ego-centric/ adult-oriented rules in order to play socially/co-operatively. Children's knowledge is expanded in the everyday conflicts and confrontations that take place between them. An example of such a development is found in the research on role-taking skills: the child's ability to perceive others as different from him/herself and act as another would. Role-taking is a social decentration. Inability to decentre limits the ability to conserve, as well as social and moral development.

Paralleling the studies of social/intellectual development described in Chapter 1, researchers such as Damon and Selman have explored decentration at social and interpersonal levels and their coincidence in intellectual decentration. The above research reinforces the Piagetian view that ego-centrism precedes a socio-centric orientation. The value of Vygotsky's (1966) work establishes the fact that once a socio-centric stage has been reached, ego-centrism does not disappear. Ego-centrism is used at various times and in various circumstances by the individual throughout life (a vital but underemphasised point in developmental theory).

Original research by Piaget (1928) on the child's ability to perceive visually from another's point of view provided information on ego-centrism and has stimulated further work on interpersonal and social perspectives. The child was shown a scale model of 'Three Mountains' from a particular angle, thus seeing a unique scene of the 'mountain range', cottages, and so on. The child was then asked to select the photographic representation of that scene from many other photographs. Upon selecting the correct photograph, the child was shown another photograph and asked where he/she would have to be to see that second scene. Results of the experiment found that children at a late sensori-motor stage (1½–2 years) could see the actual mountain as an object but were unable to perceive it in a 'symbolic' form (that is, the child was tied to the presence of the immediate object view and could not recognise the scene in a photograph). The pre-operational child was able to recognise a representation of his/her original view of the mountains, but other representations were thought not to be of the same object (the child was dominated by a personal or ego-centric view, unable to decentre). With the development of concrete operational skills, children became aware of differing visual perspectives and mastered rules and principles for their reconstruction. They could select photographs of the scene that they viewed. Additionally, they could speculate where they would need to be placed, in order to perceive the scene of another photograph. More recent research on the recognition of visual representations, such as Donaldson's, demonstrates that the more familiar the scene is for children, the earlier they are able to master differing perspectives. Donaldson used a teddy bear looking into a room in a doll's house in preference to the three mountains. Research on spatial representation generally upholds Piaget's findings but explores ambiguities of the theory of greater depth; especially of the pre-operational stage and mechanisms that hold up or promote development beyond ego-centrism.

Flavell *et al.* (1968) explored the development of role-taking and communication skills of children. Citing previous role-taking research, they noted cognitive aspects as the ability to perceive another person's role and the ability to use this knowledge to communicate more effectively. The authors proposed a model of 'Interpersonal Inference' as a guide to the acquisition of role-taking and communication skills (revised by Flavell, 1974; see Figure 2.1). Briefly, the individual must: (1) know that another possesses a certain property (Existence); (2) acknowledge that the self has use for knowledge of this property (Need); (3) have the ability to carry out this quest (Inference); (4) be capable of using the resulting information (Application). Flavell *et al.* noted that their model coincided with developing abilities in the child and that these abilities roughly paralleled the stages described by Piaget and Inhelder.

Source: Flavell, 1974, p. 71.

Figure 2.1 *Knowledge and skills involved in making inferences about other people.*

The Flavell model, more appropriately, describes how the information is processed by the individual. As the reader can see, the field of social cognition has developed into a cognitive interpretation of the understanding of people. Research on the social-cognitive abilities of children rarely explores the social context and is therefore open to accusations of incompleteness.

INTERPERSONAL UNDERSTANDING

Robert Selman's (1976a) developmental analysis of interpersonal relations is more strongly tied to social aspects of the child's life. His original research found five qualitative levels of perspective-taking 'by which the subject can structure or view interpersonal relations' between the ages of 4 and 16. The levels (p. 309) are:

Stage 0: Egocentric Viewpoint (age range 3–6)
   Child has a sense of differentiation of self and other but fails to distinguish between the social perspective (thoughts, feelings) and does not see the cause-and-effect relation of reasons to social actions.
Stage 1: Social-Informational Role-Taking (age range 6–8)
   Child is aware that other has a social perspective based on other's own reasoning, which may or may not be similar to child's. However, child tends to focus on one perspective rather than co-ordinating viewpoints.
Stage 2: Self-Reflective Role-Taking (age range 8–10)
   Child is conscious that each individual is aware of the other's perspective and that this awareness influences self and other's view of each other. Putting self in other's place is a way of judging his intentions, purposes, and actions. Child can form a co-ordinated chain of perspectives, but cannot yet abstract from this process to the level of simultaneous mutuality.
Stage 3: Mutual Role-Taking (age range 10–12)
   Child realises that both self and other can view each other mutually and simultaneously as subjects. Child can step outside the two-person dyad and view the interaction from a third-person perspective.
Stage 4: Social and Conventional System Role-Taking (age range 12–15+)
   Person realises mutual perspective-taking does not always lead to complete understanding. Social conventions are seen as necessary because they are understood by all members of the group (the generalised other) regardless of their position, role, or experience.

Selman's stages are a combination of social and role-taking ability (dependent on necessary, but not sufficient, logical operations; see Selman, 1976b, for further discussion). The stages of social perspective-taking can be seen to combine three separate aspects of development: (1) movement from ego-centric to socio-centric perspective; (2) movement through logical-mathematical stages – most obviously shown in the ability to abstract immediate personal and social experiences into an understanding of society and social conventions; (3) an underlying use of rules – from the acknowledging of individual viewpoints to the use of intention to a broad understanding of the use of social conventions. Selman has further drawn a parallel between his Social Role-Taking stages and Kohlberg's (1976) Moral Judgement stages. From this a more illuminative picture of the interaction of the child's social and intellectual world is gained.

TOWARDS A UNIFIED PERSPECTIVE

But where does this vast coverage of literature take the reader (especially when considering the dynamics and world of the primary school aged child)? The diversity of elements covered in this chapter have not been included to mystify the reader with complexities of development. A grounding in the cognitive and social-cognitive elements of social development provides more than a knowledge of stages or levels through which the child is expected to progress. All of the stages and research reviewed place the child in a socially interactive context, either by physical presence or by hypothetical dilemma. While not actually describing this social context, I would note that the perspectives developed by children are the result of interactions, primarily (as in Chapter 1) with people and then generalised into rule or object relations. Early games between infant and caretaker require the child to realise that people and objects exist outside the immediate physical and psychological realm of the child. Early interactions between caretaker and infant form a 'relationship' which has variously been described as the background for empathy and sympathy (Hoffman, 1976), all authority relationships (Dubin and Dubin, 1963) and the realisation of rules – in the morality of constraint (Piaget, 1965). Several types of play have been described for their distinctive skill (intellectual) and social qualities: the manipulation and understanding of objects practised and learned. Social relations (of dominance, with adults and children, as well as collaboration) are enacted, leading to children's understanding of their own competence. Influence of adults in direction and control of children is predominant in the early years of childhood. The peer group gains increasing influence in the middle years of childhood. Particular effects of the peer group are found in many developmental contexts illustrated in part by the conflict situations between children, which: (1) force the child to substantiate his/her own point of view (e.g. questioning); (2) provide an awareness or understanding of the self (facilitating the transition from ego-centric to social perspectives); (3) may be quantified in a knowledge and feeling for others (empathy, sympathy, altruism). Stages of perspective- and social perspective-taking as described in research by Piaget (1928, 1965), Flavell *et al.* (1968) and Selman (1976a) follow a similar pattern of development. In such a pattern the child is: (1) initially dominated by an individualistic perspective, proceeding to (2) a realisation that others have perspectives but one's own perspective still takes precedence, to (3) a relativistic realisation that each has his or her own way of seeing and using information and (4) a collaborative realisation of 'getting along' and mutual interaction with others. In a naive sense, the progression shows the child 'coming to grips' with others. This social-cognitive development can only take place as the result of the child's interactions with adults and the peer group.

A unique example of the interaction of the child with others, conscious realisation and development of mutuality was reported in Piaget's *Moral Judgement of the Child* (1965). The child's use of rules as an example of the dynamics of moral development has already been described. (Patterns of action and interactions with people within the home context have a profound effect on the structure of mental development.) Hearing and seeing rules in the environment, the child attempts to apply them him/herself. The precise understanding of these rules is bound up in the hierarchical authority relations with adults (especially parents) and co-operative relations with peers, leading to a 'morality of constraint' and a 'morality of co-operation' respectively. The authority relationships of constraint and co-operation remind us of the social context of the child's development, particularly the effects of upbringing practices and the experiences to which the child is exposed. A brief exploration of the origin of 'constraint' shows that this stage is not a simple realisation that rules are to be followed, are sacred and (usually) adult-imposed. As Piaget (1962) noted, the child's early development involves a sensory, physical, affective, social and cognitive relationship with the caretaker.

The bond between infant and caretaker which has been shown to promote intellectual development (as in object permanence of the mother) also establishes an initial authority and rule relationship. The child's dependence on adults for early physiological and physical needs (see Dubin and Dubin, 1963) corresponds closely with early understanding of rules. The child perceives rules as externally initiated, imposed and to be followed to the best of his/her understanding. While anyone who has experience with young infants will attest to the fact that children often control their parents, as noted by Bell (1968), Hoffman (1975) makes a quite categorical statement that basic physical, physiological and sensory pleasures/needs/rewards are *controlled* by parents. The relationship between child and caretaker is one of authority, but (as shown in Chapter 1) the relationship is also one of trust/dependence/security, perhaps easing the way for the acceptance of authority by the child.

The nature of the bond relationship serves as a basis for further theories of development. Within the cognitive developmental field, Hoffman (1976) has speculated that the relationship is the basis for the child's early perception of empathy. He explains that the infant must be cared for by adults in all circumstances. Circumstances include the caretaker feeling joyous or depressed (or anywhere along the scale) as well as other emotions. Being in close physical contact with the caretaker, the child has the capacity to experience physically the caretaker's internal emotional states. The infant (through a classical conditioning paradigm) becomes aware of the caretaker's bodily tension or distress and is able to alter his/her bodily state to one similar to the caretaker's. Hoffman notes the transfer of tension as empathetic distress; this serves as a basis for extended mutual feelings of empathy, sympathy and, ultimately, altruism. The theory, upon second reading, has a very firm basis in reality. Garbarino and Bronfenbrenner (1976) also use the bond relationship as a basis for their theory of moral development. Rules, for the child, are initially imposed by adults. This authoritative behaviour sets a rule relationship for early interaction with other children in play and games. But play with other children also gives rise to an alternative peer-oriented authority, often at odds with the adult-oriented authority. The adult and peer orientations of authority/rules and the child's social interactions in play around the home amply demonstrate that the child's social context, and particularly the relationships within the context, are vitally important in understanding the shaping of the child's authority development.

The early development of the 'morality of constraint' involves the child's interactions with caretaker with the underlying process of bonding. Hence, the child must interact within a relationship where rules and major decisions are made without reference to his/her desires. But the rules and decisions are made by a loved individual (affective relation). The relationship thus makes possible the acceptance of various types or levels of constraint and determines the child's reflective feelings towards this 'domination'. Recent research by William Damon has explored developmental levels of the child's realisation of the constraining relationship during the primary school years. Damon finds three distinct levels of authority and two sub-stages per level, as follows (1977, pp. 178–9).

Brief Descriptions of Early Authority Levels
Level 0-A: Authority is legitimised by attributes that link the authority figure with the self, either by establishing affectional bonds

between authority figure and self or by establishing identification between authority figure and self. The basis for obedience is a primitive association between authority's commands and the self's desires.

Level 0-B: Authority is legitimised by physical attributes of persons – size, sex, dress, and so on. The specific attributes selected are those which the subject considers to be descriptive of persons in command. These legitimising attributes may be used in a fluctuating manner, since they are not linked logically to the functioning of authority. The subject recognises the potential conflict between authority's commands and the self's wishes, and thinks about obedience in a pragmatic fashion: commands are followed as a means of achieving desires, or to avoid actions contrary to desires.

Level 1-A: Authority is legitimised by attributes which enable the authority figure to enforce his commands (physical strength, social or physical power, and so on). Obedience is based upon the subject's respect for the authority figure's social or physical power, which is invested with an aura of omnipotence and omniscience.

Level 1-B: Authority is legitimised by attributes that reflect special talent or ability, and that make the authority figure a superior person in the eyes of the subject. This special talent or ability is no longer associated simply with power, but is rather indicative of the authority figure's ability to accomplish changes that subordinates cannot. Obedience is based on reciprocal exchange: the subject obeys because the authority figure takes care of him, because the authority figure has helped him in the past, or because the authority figure otherwise 'deserves' his obedience.

Level 2-A: Authority is legitimised by prior training or experience related to the process of commanding. The authority figure is therefore seen as a person who is able to lead and command better than subordinates. Obedience is based on the subject's respect for this specific leadership ability and on the belief that this superior leadership ability implies a concern for the welfare and the rights of subordinates.

Level 2-B: Authority is legitimised by the co-ordination of a variety of attributes with specific situational factors. The subject believes that a person might possess attributes which enable him to command well in one situation but not in another. Authority, therefore, is seen as a shared, consensual relation between parties, adopted temporarily by one person for the welfare of all. Obedience is seen as a co-operative effort which is situation-specific, rather than as a general response to a superior person.

Within the progressive levels the reader will note the child's developmental realisation of this constraining authority (for instance, a realisation of a *dominant* being or rule and *submissiveness* to that person or rule; a general or particular obedience). The progression shows the child's knowledge expanding from a relationship with close affectional bonds (parental) to a more rational explanation of the relationship. The ability to explain the relationship shows an understanding of the dynamics of constraint and the child's self-realisation (or own reciprocal role) in the relationship. But the relationship and knowledge explored by Damon are based upon dominance and submission, the imposition and acceptance of constraint. Mutuality, or equality, in decision- or rule-making adds a further dimension to moral/social development.

The 'morality of co-operation' is a qualitative advancement beyond constraint. According to Piaget (1965) mutuality or equality was realised through play (and general social interaction with peers). Little research has been undertaken to explore co-operation (perhaps its very title is too ambiguous). Yet much research has experimentally centred on 'co-operative skills' to promote social-perspective-taking, cognitive skills and varying classroom regimes. A recent book by Youniss (1980) explores the intimacy, sensitivity and security of particular relations engendered in the development of friendship. With developing cognitive abilities and close friendship among peers, co-operative relations arise. Co-operation sets the background for collaboration and as such is based upon equality. Rules are not seen as externally imposed, but as agreed by and for those involved in any activity. Children who realise co-operation have an alternative to adult-oriented constraining authority. This alternative authority causes some dismay for teachers in the middle years of primary school (in classrooms of approximately 7- to 8-year-olds children would just as soon speak to one another as often as to the teacher). The realisation of mutual control in addition and/or opposition to external adult control also sets the background for the potentially 'turbulent' years of adolescence in the Western world.

Co-operation is essential to reach Piaget's moral stage of 'autonomy'; and the dynamics of heteronomy-autonomy are the basis for Kohlberg's further work on moral judgement. Both co-operation and constraint are vital for later social development. Not only do they form the authority basis for our adult social relations, they are also a basis for political development. In an ideal democracy people must co-operatively come together to vote or choose representatives who delegate authority back down on to the people. The actual balancing which allows a co-operative decision to be made in preference to a constraining decision, or vice versa, is based upon both knowledge and interaction. The balance sets the background for a social psychology of social/moral development.

The final point of importance to be drawn from Piaget's *Moral*

Judgement of the Child is that children learn by doing. The actual behavioural activities that they follow out, or are allowed to follow out, are realised by the child (as noted earlier in pre-operative and concrete schemes). One must, thereby, be aware of the actions and interactions that are allowed to occur, or are made possible, in the environment of the child. Variations between home environments will have direct behavioural implications on the amount of constraint that the child knows and expects, the number of independent actions that the child may imitate, early self-reflections of competence, and preparation to participate in co-operative activities.

The environment of the school is a prime example of an arena for interaction, behaviour and realisation which promotes the development of authority and social relations between adults and peers. The child must realise that: (1) organised knowledge exists and is transmitted through the teacher; (2) the school has a bureaucratic organisation and a system of rules or rituals (that stereotypes social relations); (3) he/she is one among many children that may be interacted with on a friendly, co-operative, or competitive basis. In exploring the actions, interactions and relationships of the primary-school-aged child, one may validly note particular effects of the social environment (co-operation *v.* competition, adult *v.* peer, constraint *v.* co-operation).

Beyond the environment of schools one may also look at cultural and cross-cultural examples. By searching outside one's culture reflective comparisons may be made. Clear examples of communal cultures are exemplified in Russia and in the life in various *kibbutzim*. (Bronfenbrenner has made extensive studies of communist and Western countries.) The use of the environmental examples of home, school and culture presents a very generalised view of situational effects on social development. One must be able adequately to explore schemes of behaviour that occur in these environments (that is, methods that the child uses to adapt to the social world) and their effect on the child's conscious or cognitive realisation.

Chapter 3

Education, Schooling and Teacher/Pupil Behaviour

EDUCATION

By the beginning of the twentieth century elementary education was compulsory for children in most Western societies. The opportunity for 'an education' had existed for a long period prior to the twentieth century, but its availability was limited to a few individuals and social classes. How education became so tied to the institutional guise of the school is a subject I shall leave to other writers and historians. The placing of education and educational responsibility in the context of the school qualifies any definition of education. An adequate concept of education must further include the philosophy of education, the aims of education, and the institutional effects (concerning the wider political nature/context and as well as the narrower context of school and classroom) and social relations of the school (from simple pupil–teacher and pupil–pupil interactions to the role and functions of administrators and bureaucracy). Not only the effect of education but the social consequences of schooling have shaped the whole of society for generations. Education may be looked upon as a process with a history, a present and a future. Education is a main transmitter of culture to succeeding generations – a key component in any definition of socialisation. This chapter will explore a range of definitions and uses of education and focus on the general process of schooling, centring on the main classroom characters of teacher and pupil.

Ignoring the social and political effects and necessities of education, the philosopher Whitehead (1964) has stated that education is the 'acquisition of the art of knowledge', Pickering (1969) has written of 'learning' and Livingstone (1941) of 'preparation': these are all 'neutral' positions on education. Such a neutral position is based upon the actual process of 'transmission' of knowledge (in some form). It is unaffected by society in general, but is rather geared towards the (basic) content of education and teaching methodologies (for example, see Plato's *Republic*, Rousseau's *Emile* and others). But the process of education not only covers the transmission of knowledge, it must also account for its subjects and schemes of internalisation – their interaction and co-ordination with the subject matter. Education is 'that process of development in which consists the passage of a human being from infancy to maturity, the process whereby the gradually adapts himself in various ways to his physical, social and spiritual environment' (Tibble, 1967, p. 15).

A further description of education places varying importance on the degree of industrial and economic 'advancement' of a particular country and the corresponding reliance on its educational system. National styles in education, along with industrial advancement, highlight the 'social engineering' for which an educational system may be employed. Industrial advancement and social engineering may best be exemplified in the Russian school system. After the Revolution the government embarked on a programme to bring literacy to the mass of the population, to create a practical technical base for Russian society (Vaizey, 1967) and to train a new generation of communal-minded youth (Bronfenbrenner, 1974).

The various definitions of education, as with socialisation, agree that it is a 'process' and point to many of the outcomes of an educational system: outcomes such as specific technical training for further industrial advancement and facilitation of social mobility. Outcomes are identifiable within the political-economic structure of a society (for a specific example see Bowles and Gintes, *Schooling in Capitalist America*, 1976). Definitions of education often have a tendency either to be too general and miss out the finer points of the system, or to be too specific and limiting. Descriptions of various roles of education and its effects (as found above) may be more appropriate and fruitful than a precise definition of education. The aim of education is slightly easier to define. Education ought to provide people with the motivation to learn and a minimum of skills necessary for life. Education does allocate both material and non-material resources of a country (Goslin, 1965). It maintains and provides examples of a common culture. This culture is responsible for the stimulation and guidance of a student's self-development mainly through its vehicle – the school. Allied with the process of intellectual advancement and learning responsibilities of the school is the provision (by example and enforcement) of a country's moral traditions. Moral traditions are often at the very root of the concept of education and schooling.

The above paragraph should not be taken to mean that education and schools are the sole vehicles for socialisation and cultural 'transmission'. One must consider primarily the structure of society (capitalist, communist, etc.), home environments and parents as the main agents of socialisation. The school's role may be seen not as secondary, but as reinforcing and expanding the primary agents of socialisation. Schools are a legitimate source of study.

Schooling and learning are ambiguous concepts in their natural environment. Attempts to understand and apply a process that may be known as 'education' have long been a debatable and often conflict-generating quest. Basic 'traditions' in education may best be exemplified as Plato's ([1961]) idealism, Rousseau's (1911) naturalism and Dewey's (1949) pragmatism. For each of the three traditions the imparting of knowledge takes place. All formulations concern the role and strength of such concepts as the school and its leading figure, the teacher. Perceptions of and planning for the child's capacity to receive and make use of information have beeen considered by educational planners within these traditions. If one looks at a society and its school/learning systems, it is rare for a single tradition to stand out as dominant. Schools are always in a 'real' situation. They interact with and are influenced by society, its moral and schooling traditions, and its historical-political-industrial context. Schooling, then, provides for social selection and promotes or hinders the advancement of individuals in any given society. The teacher bears responsibility as the conveyor of knowledge and tradition; one who carries on from the home and parents. Components in the process that is known as 'education' are thus (1) a body of knowledge and tradition to be transferred; (2) a process by which the transfer is possible, i.e. schooling; (3) an agent to be responsible for the transfer, i.e. the teacher; (4) the objects of the transfer of knowledge and tradition – the children.

SCHOOLING

The institution of the school plays a major role in the child's life from middle childhood through adolescence. Although more children are attending pre-school (or nursery) these days, the role of the primary school remains undiminished. Mandatory attendance of primary school covers the agespan during which the child makes the transition from a 'home orientation' to a 'social world orientation'. The only single activity that the child spends more time involved in than school between the ages of 5 and 16 is sleeping; although television is fast asserting itself. In sheer quantity of time, the school asserts itself as a major agency in the socialisation of the child. The school is, generally, charged with the transfer of knowledge and traditions of a society to its children. Its charge serves as an initial insight into the tensions of the school; for the charge is a major paradox. While the school transfers a set and existing body of information it must also provide for the encouragement and implementation of change (Goslin, 1965).

The school also functions as an allocator of status. It can channel occupational desires and skills and carry a prestige about itself. Prestige and impact of socialisation are important products of schooling, as has been pointed out by Himmelweit and Swift (1969). They further state that there should be more adequate studies of schooling and its socialising effects, for the school is part of the 'child's total interaction'. While the educational system is meant to provide the rudiments of literacy and numeracy for all children, schools have been shown to maintain a specific 'ethos' (see Sharp and Green, 1976). Ethos is a certain identity (in its control of pupils, relations among staff members, relationships to the community, etc.) characteristic of each individual school. In referring to ethos, it is certainly difficult to generalise about schools. Distinctive differences can be found in the outcome of schooling (attendance, behaviour, examination results) when similarly structured schools drawing pupils from the same community are compared (see Rutter *et al.*, 1979). Schools are also charged with the social, moral and, at times, religious education of their pupils.

The various stages of schooling emphasise different aspects of education. The primary school places weight on skill and social training. The secondary school stresses expansion and integration of broad areas of knowledge. Tertiary education emphasises occupational, academic training and initiation into adult life-style. The school, though, is not an entity that stands outside the mainstream of society. The social influences of the home and the peer group must be met and contended with in the school.

The structure of the educational system and its application through the school necessitate that the institution (the school) not only provides for the cognitive advancement of the child, but serves additionally as a 'teacher' of 'norms' (or social rules of behaviour with specific content and methods for acceptance; see Dreeban, 1967). For many children the primary school is their first formal experience outside the home. It maintains and exaggerates the intellectual and socialising roles. The school may be looked upon as a main arena for moral/social experience. It provides the intellectual and social experiences and information for the child through many teaching and learning styles. The styles may vary with school ethos, teacher orientation and subject matter. But the conveying of school knowledge remains essentially a social interaction between child and teacher. The teacher's character in schooling takes on the dual role of member and manipulator of the classroom. The childhood community within the school shows initial dependence on the teacher, perceiving her/him as similar (in resemblance and identification and nurturance) to the parent (as reported by the Plowden Commission, 1967). It is not unusual for a child in the first year of school to ask 'Will you tie my shoe, Mummy?' This slip of words is used in the presence of any adult in the classroom (male or female). The teacher is also a purveyor of knowledge (Morrison and McIntyre, 1969).

Both knowledge and teacher may all too easily be presented and passed off as controlling elements/figures whose authority is similar to Piaget's (1965) morality of constraint. The analogy is not far from the point. Experiences in the arena of the school may either expand or limit actual behaviours of the child and thereby have great importance for that child's social and intellectual development. (Behavioural experiences, especially social behavioural experiences, are the foundation for the social/moral development.) But it would be naive to suggest that the teacher or other school authority figures are the only, or main, interactionists in the child's schooling experience. The child's social behaviours also arise in interaction with the peer group.

The classroom in the school provides a stable structure for the child to build a system of 'mutual friends' (Glidewell *et al.*, 1966), i.e. a peer group. The effect of groups in the learning and expansion of thought through interaction is a much-documented area. The overt effect of groups is the creation of friendships and group norms (Evans, 1962). The peer group has been put to effective use in character education in the USSR school system, as noted by Bronfenbrenner (1974). (The outcome of the Russian venture was a training in the communist tradition and a swing away from the formalistic teacher-centred educational system; see Fraser, 1964.) Opposed to the conscious shaping of the child's social thought is the American orientation to schooling. The American child is prepared for decision-making, thus avoiding separate courses in moral education (leaving only experience to dictate the social development of its youth). Piaget (1971) noted that the peer group also promotes the cognitive conflict necessary for expansion of thought through play and discussion. Growth of influence of the peer group is associated (in the West) with increasing independence for the child and corresponding tension towards adult authority figures (Gesell and Ilg, 1965). Games and social interactions with peers provide the experiences necessary to apply and adjust rules for a *co-operative* morality. Schools use children in leadership roles (in sport, room movements, etc.) and provide both practical and educational experience of political socialisation. The process of schooling then is both instrumental and *expressive* of a specific culture (Bernstein, 1960). School ethics, climate and modes of interaction all have effects on the development of, and future possibilities for, the pupil.

Schooling, in summary, covers a broad area of intellectual and social behavioural socialisation. The process takes place under the direction and domination of the main agent of the school – its teacher. Given the social development that takes place in the school, that is, the formation of the peer group and individual identity, competence, etc., we must further explore the processes of social and intellectual effects of education. The study of education and its formal concept of schooling must include the effects that the teacher has upon the pupil and the reaction of the pupil to the teacher and to peers during continuing intellectual and social development.

TEACHER BEHAVIOUR

The role and effects of education through the eighteenth and nineteenth centuries have been traced in England by Thompson (1963). In its present form the role of the teacher was established in England during the Middle Ages under the auspices of the church. Utilisation of the teacher in mass education did not achieve its present socially powerful position until the 1870s when education was first made compulsory. Grace (1979) provides further information and a background for an ideological construction of the teacher's role. His review of the urban teacher concludes that the teacher is 'caught up in a massive apparatus of control'.

Aside from his/her social and intellectual roles in education, the teacher also fulfils the economic function of social selection and allocation in industrialised societies (Wilson, 1962). Industrial expansion leads to further specialisation of the teacher and subject matter, and an increasing importance for teacher judgements and recommendations for pupils' courses and their futures.

In the above constraints, the teacher's understanding and concept of his/her role in the educational system is subject to many conflicts according to Hoyle (1969). The teacher must present a specialised knowledge to the pupils (who come from different backgrounds and industrial orientations and have varying needs to be fulfilled by the educational system). He/she must act as a model for all. The teacher also finds him/herself in conflict with parents and parental expectations, the hierarchy of the school (heads of departments and headmasters), education administration and other personnel. A further constraint in the teacher's realm may be termed a national climate of schooling. The national climate may be characterised in the move from traditional to progressive in post-Plowden primary schools and the present call for a stronger *basic* curriculum. Galton, Simon and Croll (1980) point out that the primary school teacher of today is in a very contradictory situation. Given the massive number of constraints on the teacher the addition of the classroom researcher would seem minor; but it is of great importance to us as it helps illuminate specific effects of teacher and school on the development of the child.

The teacher him/herself derives the concept of the particular role from classroom experiences, previous education, reading and job training, which is more fully explained by Dunkin and Biddle (1974). The teacher's role is, according to Hoyle (1969), to instruct, socialise and facilitate or teach motivation. The teacher must structure curriculum and behaviour and serve as a model for growth and development.

He/she mediates between the child and society during school hours. He/she has responsibility for transferring social effects and behaviours to the pupil and (Musgrove and Taylor, 1969) is thereby expected to assume both the 'intellectual and instrumental roles'. The teacher becomes a 'servant of the state' (Russell, 1951), which expects him/her to carry on the traditions of its culture. Traditions, it must be remembered, are moral as well as intellectual and social. (Moral education, whether taught as a separate subject or incorporated into teaching style and curriculum, has long been a province of the primary school. It further emphasises the teacher's role in providing for the intellectual and social development of the pupil.)

Classroom procedure shows the teacher to be both 'policeman and judge' (Morrison and McIntyre, 1969). The teacher's actual role leaves him/her in an ill-defined position, open to conflicting expectations. The resolution of the ambiguities is most often left to the individual teacher, laying undue stress on his/her background, expectations and classroom experience. While the teacher is in a position of responsibility and control, Grace points out that his/her role is 'never entirely determined by' the constraints imposed on the position. The teacher brings individual characteristics to the classroom.

As the teacher's role varies with expectations, so too do teaching styles. According to Galton *et al.* (1980), teaching styles vary a great deal from traditional to progressive methods, dependent on teacher and pupil need. More individual styles incorporate reflective, analytic and artistic teaching methods. Styles vary with the differing age-groups taught, localities in which the teaching situation takes place, ethos of the school and the teacher's own interpretation of classroom learning.

Teachers' attitudes and, possibly, prejudices are based upon individual backgrounds and the school community. Differences between teachers have been found by Hoyle to be based on age, experiences in schools, sex, attitudes towards application of authority and type of school. Overwhelmingly, teachers come from a middle-class background and often another member of the immediate family is also a teacher (see Morrison and McIntyre, 1969). But teachers' orientations to schools are not totally pre-set by background. Butcher (1965) found that teachers' classroom attitudes are formed over time, and in relation to the teaching situation. Training teachers, according to Butcher, are more 'naturalistic', 'radical' and 'tenderminded' than those in full-time teaching positions. But attitudes 'liberalise' after three or four years of teaching and may be reversed in the longer term. (While Butcher used different samples in a cross-sectional methodology for his study, Cortis, 1970, found similar results in a longitudinal study, along with distinctions between primary and secondary teachers.)

The different social communities that feed a particular school will be reflected in parental and child expectations of school (achievement, attainment, acceptance, rejection, phobias, etc.). Rutter *et al.*'s (1979) study of inner London secondary schools amply demonstrates the wide range of pupils that go to most comprehensive schools. Schools do respond to their communities but also present a general ethos based on the cumulative effects of various social factors.

Principles which guide the running, atmosphere and identity of a school and classroom have been studied by Sharp and Green in their (1976) exploration of school ethos. The ethos of a school is not simply a name or label applied to a type of education; it is more pervasive. As Rutter *et al.* point out, an ethos is more than the sum of the social and ideological factors in and around the school. Ethos is a 'feel' about a school by which people in the school interact and the school becomes known in the community. An ethos is most easily identifiable in a primary school, basing itself on formal or progressive principles. In primary schools the ethos is often determined by the head, who has a large say in the hiring of teachers and in the structure and day-to-day activities of the school. It is more difficult to pinpoint the origin of the ethos of a secondary school. Secondary ethos minimally may be seen as the sum of institutional effects which have far-reaching consequences for the pupil and school. Similarity of design and organisational structure between schools provides no basis for a common ethos. An ethos is evident in life beyond secondary education, influencing qualifications, job availability and university placement.

Although evidence for the existence of ethos is strong, Sharp and Green emphasise that it is the individual teacher who examines, interprets and applies it in her/his own classroom. Interpretation and application by the teacher set a classroom *climate* (of warmth or coldness) and management *style* (of greater or lesser directiveness). Effects of the climate and style generally dictate patterns of pupil learning (to be discussed later). The studies *Teacher Styles and Pupil Progress* (Bennett, 1976) and its reanalysis (Aitken *et al.*, 1981) and *Inside the Primary Classroom* (Galton *et al.*, 1980) demonstrate general school ethos while showing that individual teachers vary in their classroom interpretation of the ethos: differential pupil performance is the main result of this variation.

Thus far this section has presented an overview of teacher behaviours, some of the constraints on the individual teacher and very broad classroom effect. The remainder will specifically explore classroom behaviours and interaction with pupils.

Studies of pupil–teacher interaction help to describe the role played by the teacher in the school. While children must interact with the teacher, the dominant or power position in which the teacher places him/herself over the child is important for understanding the impact of the teacher. The general classroom atmosphere is a determinant in both the amount of work accomplished and the initial application of authoritarian and democratic attitudes (e.g. political socialisation) for the child (Morrison and McIntyre, 1969). Effects of the teacher's activities and attitudes have been noted initially and most forcefully in Rosenthal and Jacobson's (1968) study of the self-fulfilling prophecy. While results from this original study have not been fully replicated, many aspects of teacher expectation have been found to affect pupils (see Brophy and Good, 1974, for a full discussion). Considering that teachers have several hundred interpersonal contacts with pupils per day (Jackson, 1968), it may be wise to point out some of the effects. In their review Brophy and Good note a combination of psychological and practical classroom issues. Examples of studies cited are:

(1) Differences in social class of teacher and pupil.
   (a) Brown *et al.* (1969) found that middle-class teachers interacted as much with middle-class as with working-class children, but were generally more positive and facilitative with middle-class children.
   (b) Teachers of lower-class pupils have been found to be less warm and positive than teachers of middle-class pupils (Yee, 1968).
(2) Teachers tend to prefer passive and conforming pupils – as noted in ratings of pupil descriptions by student teachers (Feshback, 1969) and supported in further studies such as Good and Grouws (1972).
(3) Physical attractiveness affects teachers' perception of pupils (Dion *et al.*, 1972).
(4) Expectancy effects have been supported in the quality of interactions with high-expectancy pupils (Davis and Levine, 1970), ability groupings in classrooms (Douglas, 1964) and teacher awareness of older siblings (Seaver, 1971).
(5) Attributional effects – teachers have been found to maintain an initial judgement (e.g. primary effect) of the child although the child's behaviour may have changed over time (Murray *et al.*, 1972; Jones *et al.*, 1968).
(6) Modelling and reinforcement effects.
   (a) Krosier and De Vault (1967) found the teacher was an authority figure with whom the (young) child could easily identify.
   (b) With the use of praise and positive reinforcement children's behaviour can be altered – but the teacher must be aware that both pro-social and anti-social behaviours can be reinforced (see Hall *et al.*, 1968; Mussen and Eisenberg-Berg, 1977).

Most of the studies cited above were undertaken in the United States, but principles of the teacher–pupil relationships have cross-cultural implications, particularly for Britain. However, it should be noted that the studies were undertaken within an American cultural context.

Early studies concerning classroom interaction draw out the cultural context of the research. Since the Second World War many observational studies of teacher and child behaviour in the United States have explored the *democratic* and *non-authoritarian* qualities of teachers (Delamont, 1976). Anderson and Brewer (1946) and Anderson, Brewer and Reed (1946) developed an observation schedule noting dominative and integrative behaviours of teachers in interactions with their pupils. Results showed most teachers to have both dominative and integrative qualities with their use dependent on classroom situations. Particular recommendations for methods of classroom control and management (Kounin, 1970) have been a result of these early observational studies. By focusing on verbal interaction, Flanders (1970) explored direct and indirect teacher influence using the Flanders Interaction Categories schedule. (The importance of the FIAC is demonstrated by the sheer amount of research arising from, and adaptations of, the original schedule.) An underlying principle of the schedule was that the more *indirect* the teacher's influence, the more democratic the process of learning was to be. Uses of the FIAC have included: (1) exploration of appropriate teaching methods for particular pupils, where dependent-prone pupils achieved better classroom results with a directive teacher, independent pupils achieved better results with non-directive teachers (Amidon and Flanders, 1961); (2) developmental changes in amount and type of teacher behaviours over the years of elementary education, from nurturant and indirect influences of the 1st grade teacher to a more direct and dominating role for the teacher of older children (Furst and Amidon, 1967). Much criticism has been levelled at the FIAC (Stubbs and Delamont, 1976), but most of it is tied to inappropriate use of the observational schedule. The FIAC has its limitations in that it does not account for general classroom content, interpretation of verbal exchanges, non-verbal interactions (such as expressions, gestures, etc.) and the history of the classroom. The use of observation schedules such as the FIAC must be limited by the appropriate method for the individual schedule (to be discussed further in the next chapter). In partial answer to the above criticism, more adequate observation methods should be used. Some advances in observational methods include: Delamont's (1976) study of a girls' private school which initially used an FIAC but also accounted for physical setting, personal appearance, pupil opinion of each teacher and recorded dialogues, and showed teacher effectiveness to be a combination of the above aspects; and Adelman and Walker (1975), who emphasised the total content of the classroom in their observation study. Other researchers, such as Galton *et al.*

(1980), have used other observational systems to gain greater insight into the dynamics of primary school classrooms.

But let us step back from the observational and methodological aspects of teacher and classroom behaviour. The earlier statement that most teachers come from above-average homes (Morrison and McIntyre, 1969) points to numerous areas of potential conflict between teacher and child. Some indication of conflict was gained in the expectation sudies cited earlier, and it is brought to the fore in circumstances such as when the pupil must choose courses (for certificates) and actual career opportunities. The teacher must provide guidance, and thereby is again in a position of constraint. The conflict between teacher and pupil is clearly brought out in studies of classroom language. Early research by Bernstein (1960) noted different speech 'codes' that he claimed were characteristic of the working and middle classes. I shall not attempt to summarise Bernstein's contributions or the very powerful criticisms and qualifications of his research (see Rosen, 1972; Labov, 1973; Barnes, 1976; Cooper 1976). It should be emphasised that the *restricted* and *elaborated* characterisation of individual speech and relations was only proportionally (not exclusively) related to social classes. The use of one code or the other did not correlate with (cognitive) intelligence. The extension of Bernstein's research to the classroom provided an account of conflict between teacher (of middle class) and child (of working class). Middle-class teachers are more likely to use elaborated code speech. These teachers will often be at linguistic and educational odds with children from working-class backgrounds. Again this research has been qualified, especially in that Bernstein has underemphasised the amount of *restricted* control of classrooms by teachers.

Stubbs (1976) expands on the types of control inherent in teacher talk in his exploration of types of classroom language. Types of language are:

Attention or showing attention
Controlling amount of speech or confirming understanding
Checking
Summarising
Defining
Editing
Correcting
Specifying topic
Keeping children on the topic.

These types of language support Morrison and McIntyre's (1969) qualification (from children's perceptions) of teacher as judge and policeman. Language, then, is a basic mode for conveying a teacher's authority in the classroom. Particular techniques of question-asking enforce or reinforce the teacher's position and patterns of child learning (e.g. knowledge as transmission or actively constructed and facilitated through the use of closed or open-ended questions; see Barnes, 1976, for further discussion). According to Docking (1980) control and order are central to the awareness of the role and conflicts of teachers, from the probationer to the most experienced practitioner. Control is central in the teacher's self-definition and sets a background for the understanding of individuals and groups of pupils.

Through language, interaction and general attitude the teacher does have a role in shaping pupils' awareness of themselves. Nash (1973) found that the teacher's perception of the pupils' social and intellectual standing in a classroom was a determining factor in the formation of classroom cliques in a top junior classroom (11-year-olds). Cliques were not based on the social class of the pupils. Groupings were based on pupils' perceptions of their teacher's perceptions of themselves. Hence, classroom groupings ranged from academically/behaviourally good children, to good behaviour/low ability and to badly behaved children. Further, the clique formation was dependent on the particular teacher. Cliques changed when the children graduated to a new teacher in a new school. The principle of pupil perception of teacher perception remained the same.

Particular attitudes and behaviours of the teacher can help in the education of particular pupils. Evidence shows greater sensitivity and, hence, greater learning of dependent-prone pupils when taught by a directive teacher (Amidon and Flanders, 1961); moulding of divergent thinking abilities by an informal classroom situation (Haddon and Lytton, 1969); and a reflective teacher effecting a reflective change in a pupil's approach to learning over the school year (Yando and Kagan, 1968). The effective teacher will structure the environment of the classroom and learning experience for the pupils as well as setting an intellectual and social model for them.

This discussion of teacher behaviour has explored the background and assertion of the teacher's role. It is useful to point out that teacher behaviour is often in response to the school and classroom situation. Hannam, Smyth and Stephenson (1976) interestingly acknowledge that young teachers' style (and control) results from expectations by pupils as well as colleagues.

Teachers must be aware of the beneficial and detrimental effects of their behaviour. The teacher, then, is a powerful agent in the administration of education. Surely the teacher's model presents a strong influence in the shaping of the child's intellectual and social behaviours: an influence with which the child can and does identify. The teacher is the figure responsible for introducing the child into the social world of the school. The teacher must be aware of the total effect that he or she has upon the pupil. Expectation and prejudice, too, shape the child's view of life.

CHILD CLASSROOM BEHAVIOUR

Knowing the role of the teacher and the many effects he/she has upon the pupil, one receives a rather one-sided view of educational development. The essential feature of the educational system is that the learning, internalisation, or adaptation process allows culture to be transmitted through the generations. The child plays an active part in this socialisation process by the very fact that he/she is going to school. Apart from the intellectual training that he/she receives, sub-culture patterns which help form the child's self-perceptions of status and role are active components of the educational system (Elkin and Handel, 1960). The school provides a character or social education for the child, where (as in Russia) she/he learns the morality of the peer group, self-discipline and responsibility.

During the child's development through school years, one notices the varying effects of the school's environment on the child. The Plowden Report viewed the child in the primary school as a pool of ability, shaped through the socialising effects of educational and social growth. Gesell and Ilg (1965) describe the normal growth pattern of child behaviour from 5 to 10 years of age. Their findings show a pattern of development from the mother/parent-centred home to peer-centred social relations. The role of teacher and the school appeared in the middle of the transition from the home to peer group.

In school, the teacher was seen initially as a parental figure, then as a teaching figure (of intellectual expertise) different from the parent (but an adult as opposed to another child), and finally as a figure of discipline and classroom authority. The development and understanding of a teacher is aptly demonstrated in the following quotations taken from conversations between children and myself.

Self:	Can you tell me about teachers?
Neil (aged 4):	They are nice . . . they tie your shoes . . . they teach you to read and write . . . teach you poems.
Self:	How did you know that?
Neil:	'Cos I go to school.
Janet (aged 6):	They put writing on the board and you've got to copy it.
Self:	Do they do anything else?
Janet:	They give you work to read.

Younger children's understanding of the teacher was a basic description of classroom activities. Most children liked their teacher for no apparent reason. Older children expanded their concept of a teacher:

Jane (aged 7):	They tell children to be good and carry on with their work.
Self:	Do you like the teacher?
Jane:	Yes. Because, if we didn't we wouldn't get a job when we grow up.
Michael (aged 9):	Well, they teach you sums and teach us all sorts . . . and now and then they just tell you off.

Apart from classroom experiences, the teacher is also seen as a disciplinarian. With even older children the concept of a teacher is further expanded. Discipline and liking are qualified:

Anita (aged 11):	They teach you about history . . . and they tell you off which I think is good because it helps you behave . . . I like them because they are helpful. If we didn't have teachers there wouldn't be anything, really, that we could do; because we wouldn't be able to add up or anything like that.

The teacher's similarity to the parent enables the child to identify with the teacher as both a behavioural authority and an intellectual example. The relevance of teacher identity is dictated by the pupil's position in the schooling process; for instance, there is less identity/affinity with teacher as the pupil approaches school-leaving age (Wright, 1962). The teacher does serve as a model in the schooling process whose role in the classroom provides information, judges classroom behaviours and uses behavioural shaping mechanisms to motivate the child to learn. Children are well aware of the teacher and teacher's role. Nash (1976), using an adaptation of Kelley's (1955) technique to elicit constructs, found six basic bipolar constructs by which pupils perceive teachers. The constructs were:

Keep order	Unable to keep order
Teaches you	Doesn't teach you
Explains	Doesn't explain
Interesting	Boring
Fair	Unfair
Friendly	Unfriendly

The constructs do provide evidence that children are well aware of the role and tensions of teachers described earlier. In Docking's (1980) review of studies of children's perceptions of teachers, consistent preference was expressed for teachers who controlled pupils' behaviour. Children also wished for some freedom to express their individuality. Children did not like a *soft* teacher. Interviews with children reveal that children prefer a teacher who is both intellectually and socially/emotionally supportive.

The teacher's classroom presence has been described by teachers and pupils as a controlling presence. Measures of the control have been noted in the teacher's behaviour and expectations of pupils. Pupils' perceptions of teacher's perceptions have been discussed in the formation of cliques (see Nash, 1973). Both teacher behaviour and classroom structure (whether streamed or mixed-ability) affect pupils' self-concept and self-esteem. During the school years children's judgements of themselves academically are based upon teacher assessment. Academic self-esteem is a large part of general self-esteem (see Coopersmith, 1967). Generation of self-concept and self-esteem and the role of the school are thoroughly reviewed by Burns (1979). Teachers' perceptions and labelling of pupils' behaviour often leads to further development of that behaviour by children, especially in the creation of school deviancy (studied by Eggleston, 1979). Deviant acts in the classroom are *created* to the extent that they are labelled by the teacher and children are identified with these acts. Classroom peer groups often promote and support the occurrence of the deviant acts.

The peer group in the infant school is largely an ineffectual gathering of pupils who are greatly dependent on the parents and the teacher, as described by Gesell and Ilg and the Plowden Commission. Through the junior school the pupils begin interacting with other pupils as well as with the teacher. Behavioural activities of children within infant and junior schools may seem outwardly similar throughout the age-range, but underlying meanings of the behaviours are qualitatively different. (As an example, the sheer amount of speech may be the same for a 5-year-old and a 10-year-old, but the proportion of social speech (see Chapter 2) will be much greater for the older child.) The peer group in the junior school is often overlooked as a socialising influence (Hartup, 1968). Studies by Kemp (1955) and Flanders and Haviemaki (1960) have shown the interaction in the school among pupils to be partially determined by IQ and socioeconomic status, as well as favourable and unfavourable perception by the teacher (Nash, 1973) and teacher expectation of intelligence (Rosenthal and Jacobson, 1968). The peer group itself is able to present a cohesive learning structure which (on the social level) can impose its own system of rewards and sanctions. The peer group poses a potentially conflicting situation for teachers and pupils in the junior school classroom. A most pointed example of pupil–teacher conflict comes at the time when the child's socialised speech expands to include a peer (in addition to adult) orientation. Children (roughly between 6 and 8 years) will talk to other children as much as they will talk to adults. Classroom indiscipline is a likely result. Conflict among peers, as previously noted in Chapter 2, promotes cognitive development through discussion and questioning (Piaget, 1971). Peers also provide the experiences necessary to apply and adjust rules for a 'co-operative' morality through games and social interactions.

Conflicts between the child's wanting to become part of the peer group and remaining loyal to the teacher became increasingly evident between 7 and 9 years of age. Further, development from 9 years onwards formalises the role of the peer group. The child makes particular and strong friendships among other children. The children's social life can become progressively divorced from the school (although peer groupings often assert themselves in and around secondary schools, as shown in separate studies by Hargreaves, 1967, and Lacey, 1970). As previously pointed out, schoolchildren/adolescents quickly form friendship cliques which correlate to their perceived positions in school. Cliques vary from strongly school-oriented, to out-of-school or anti-school orientations, with several intermediary orientations. Cliques appear to support the existence of the two teacher roles of educator and disciplinarian. The peer group presents a challenge to teachers in that it will support its members' behaviour, especially in the challenge to teacher authority in secondary schools (see Willis, 1977, and others). The existence of the school is responsible for the introduction and formation of the peer group.

The child's growth from the home through the school years also emphasises the conflict between parent and teacher (Morrison and McIntyre, 1969). The conflict is represented in a study of the child's conception of ego ideal, which is generally most similar to the parent, but incorporates specific aspects of the teacher (Wright, 1962). The teacher is seen by the child in the early years of schooling as a parental substitute from whom praise and encouragement is sought. Children in reception classes, while concentrating on the work of the moment, often call their teacher 'Mummy'. The child is able to interact with a teacher much the same as with individual parents. Behaviours such as deviance are found in both the home and the school (Mitchell and Shepard, 1966). But parental and teacher dependence is negatively related to dependence on the peer group (McCandless *et al.*, 1961) and conflicts do arise. Findings such as above which illuminate potential conflicts between home and school, parent and teacher, and among peers, provide insight into the generation of 'deviant' behaviours learnt in and around schools (see Marsh *et al.*, 1978).

Given that the teacher must be aware of the child and his/her behaviours, one can find reasons for many of the deviance problems that manifest themselves in the classroom – the child's actions and the teacher's reactions (documented as long ago as 1928 by Wickman).

The child appears to follow a certain growth pattern in his/her advancement into the social world. This advancement can largely be determined by teacher modelling roles which, inevitably, will affect future child behaviours and perceptions. Bronfenbrenner (1974) extends this thesis by drawing upon the individual *v.* collective patterns of schooling and classroom structure (as well as child-rearing) in the United States and Russia.

CONCLUSION

The formal process of education (which includes a concept of schooling and the interactional patterns between teacher and pupil) describes the child's transition from the home to society at large. In this transition to the social world the child is being shaped by the socialisation processes of the school and teacher. Schooling, which can shape society's children into a particular social ethic, is characteristic of the country in which it is taking place. As with the teaching of intellectual materials, social habits and behaviours are also transferred to the child in the school. The child's awareness and ability to internalise information is dependent on his/her developing psychological structures. The social and intellectual information provided in the school and classroom environment will have profound effects on the developing child. The teacher who serves as model and provider of information must arrange for the process accordingly, while being aware of the effect that he/she is having upon the child. On the social level, the child gains a developing awareness of the peer group (which does not exert its power until the late junior school) and uses the teacher as a transitional figure of authority and introduction into the peer group society. The child's perception of the teacher varies through the steps of this social transition. The teacher, too, changes in job responsibility and classroom methods in this period of middle childhood. The school, classroom, teacher and pupil provide an arena, circumstances, form and interactors necessary for development and evaluation. Chapter 4 will discuss an approach (and methodology) that brings together this diverse body of literature into a more cohesive understanding of the role and effect of the teacher and peer group in primary education.

Chapter 4

Methodological and Study Considerations

SOCIALISATION

The literature covered in Chapters 1, 2 and 3 has provided a broad background to early social and intellectual development, the middle years of childhood and the role and function of the school (with its characters of teacher and pupil). I have not consciously avoided the term 'socialisation', which has often been used to describe these developments; rather, in reviewing the aspects of development and the school, I have described and discussed many of the essential elements that would combine to make an adequate theory of socialisation. There are many definitions of socialisation. One of the most comprehensive of these is Brim's (1966, p. 3): 'the process by which individuals acquire the knowledge, skills and dispositions that enable them to participate as more or less effective members of groups and the society'. Socialisation is not a simple initiation into society. There are particular skills and areas of knowledge to be trained in and made aware of. There are párticular people with whom to interact. All of these *behaviours* take place within a social context. An adequate theory of socialisation would include: (1) a process, an ongoing pattern and realisation of interaction; (2) a history of individual and social development; (3) a history of cultural and societal development; (4) particular attributes in the form of rules and sanctions characteristic of a society (or any part of it); (5) intellectual as well as social advancement; (6) agents or individuals with whom to interact.

In the literature reviewed, definite elements of socialisation have been described. But there is a contradiction in any definition of socialisation; for while the definition may be descriptive of the many elements of socialisation, the actual dynamics can only be hinted at. To serve the purposes of this chapter I shall draw on two theoretical orientations to provide insight into the dynamics of socialisation and a basis for the methodology of the ensuing study. Denzin (1977) has recently applied *symbolic interactionist theory* to childhood socialisation. This theory is drawn from the philosophy and research of Mead (1964), Goffman (1967) and others. Denzin emphasises the roles of interpersonal interaction and negotiation within a social frame (a qualification of Goffman), focusing on symbolic (gestural) and linguistic forms of natural behaviour. Symbolic interactionist theory notes the sophistication of the process by which individuals achieve understanding. Knowledge is not just given and accepted. Individuals bring their backgrounds and expectations into interaction. It is through symbolic forms that discussion, compromise, development and change take place. Denzin has studied using children's games and language, anecdotes and provided contextual explanations for and interpretations of their development. (If criticism may be levelled at Denzin, it would focus on his misinterpretation of Piaget as an age-deterministic, maturational theorist, and his restricted use of cognitive developmental theory.) *Cognitive developmental theory* (perhaps most adequately described by Kohlberg, 1969) similarly accounts for interactions between the individual and others (including objects). It encompasses development of the social and intellectual self. It is based upon actions (gestural, linguistic and behavioural). But cognitive developmental theory also provides for a personal/developmental history which must account for specific environmental and cultural influences. While specific stages of development are often related to ages of children, the relationship of stage to age is only approximate. It is experience that is necessary for stage development.

OUTLINE FOR THE STUDY: A DEVELOPMENTAL ORIENTATION

The study to be described in the remaining sections of this book is rooted in the above theories and focuses on the primary school. The school has previously been described as an agency of socialisation and of prime transitionary importance in the child's advancement from a family home orientation into a fuller social and community context. Formally, the school provides for intellectual advancement and cultural transmission. Informally, the child is introduced to a teacher (with parent-like and expert qualities) and a multitude of peers. Formally, again, the child must act and interact with people representing the archetypical authority relations (of hierarchical constraint and mutual co-operation) within an institutionalised and bureaucratic setting. With the development of intellectual knowledge/understanding comes social knowledge/understanding. The context and role of the school provide (additionally) for moral/social/political development and differentiation. While the above has referred mainly to development, the child's intellectual and social competence are also assessed in the school. The primary school provides a forum or arena for development and practise of intellectual/social schemes, rules and knowledge.

Development is impossible to define precisely. Instances and types of development have been discussed in Chapters 1 and 2, from which the following points are drawn. All development has its basis in actions of the individual, which include behaviour, language, symbols and abstract thought. There are strong parallels between intellectual, social and moral thought, as exemplified in the stages of interpersonal understanding (reviewed by Shantz, 1975) and the limitation of the stage of moral judgement due to intellectual ability (Kohlberg, 1976). A simple example of intellectual-moral limitation may be seen in the advent of intention in moral thought. Most adults would attribute moral thinking to children's explanations of their bad behaviour. The ability to explain incorporates the understanding that the individual previously knew that the behaviour was wrong and proceeded with it anyway. The ability to explain is linked with *intention*. But children's earliest explanations are usually made after the behaviour took place: they are rationalisations. The behaviour leading to explanation is an example of pre-operative thought. It is quite a different and advanced mode of thinking to apply an explanation before the behaviour. Intention requires advance planning, not just descriptive rationalisation after an event (an example of social conservation).

Development has been described as a 'dialectic of personal growth' (Baldwin, 1906, p. 9), a 'self-constructive process' (Turiel, 1969, p. 95) and essentially a matter of action and cognitive mediation in which 'the initial and end conditions are behaviour' (Youniss, 1978, p. 207). While the actions are personal (to the individual), there are certain underlying common experiences in social and intellectual development. Commonalities have been shown in development through social role-taking (Selman, 1976b), social development (Piaget, 1959), moral development (Piaget, 1965), and so on. On the one hand, we must be wary not to adopt an over-cognitive view of development. On the other hand, children's individual free and spontaneous actions provide common cognitive/behavioural elements. In their studies both Hoffman (1975, 1976) and Youniss (1978) note that individual families have their own styles of child-rearing, discipline, and so on, but there are also common moral constraints (parental power) and social perspectives (autistic, ego-centric, socio-centric) that the child adopts.

Youniss cites Piaget's *Moral Judgement of the Child* as a major work on social development. He focuses on seven main points from the book (1978, pp. 211–13):

(1) Children are born into a network of social relations in which they hold several positions.
(2) Once the child has achieved the concept of permanence of things and of persons outside him or herself, others begin to play a direct role in the construction of order.
(3) Order is derived from interactions when the child constructs rule systems, or relations.

(4) The division of self from others according to relational rule systems is required if children are to order themselves within existing social networks.

(5) Any relation can be observed to develop in the sense that one or both parties can reconstruct themselves with respect to the other.

(6) Throughout development . . . there is an advantage to considering self and others . . . as relativistic concepts.

(7) Conceptions of persons . . . are open to change as relations themselves develop.

While the above points are essential to a cognitive view of social development, one needs to qualify and add the following: (*a*) Piaget (1965) also points out the archetypical authority relations of constraint and co-operation, and the action-based Law of Conscious Realisation; (*b*) the roots of moral/authority relations lie in the sensory-motor-affective schemes of infancy (Piaget, 1951), and these roots focus on the limited but powerful caretaker/attachment effects (these points have been discussed in Chapter 2).

To summarise the cognitive developmental perspective, the child is seen as an active organiser (Damon, 1977) of experience. He/she appears as a rule-making and rule-following animal (Hogan, 1973). Rules are adapted by the child through interactions of present and advancing knowledge, behaviours (physical, verbal) and the context within which the action takes place. Furth (1978) proposes four stages of societal understanding (in children 6–11 years of age) which draw together social/intellectual, rules and understanding of money, society and social regulations. The stages are:

(1) playful;
(2) functional – playful understanding of immediately served functions;
(3) part-systemic – extension of above through personal aspects;
(4) systemic-concrete – a rudimentary understanding of society functions.

As the reader will see, there is a strong cognitive developmental underpinning to societal understanding. The child actively participates in the surrounding social/societal context. As with intention, the developing ability to understand and conceptualise forms the basis for the individual's interaction in society.

In studying aspects of games and rules one must be aware of the interactional and intellectual aspects and the constraints of participants and environment. Piaget acknowledges the constraining power of parents in early moral/authority development and social relations. Denzin also points to the apparent freedom of games and play. But these behaviours take place within the (contradictory) constraints of the social/rule-bound environment. Rule knowledge is an authority in its own right.

We are now able to bring into focus the multiple topics and points of interest in this social and developmental psychological study of the primary school. The study reported in Chapter 5 follows the behavioural interactions with, and verbal knowledge of, authority patterns between children, their teachers and their peers. In developing social knowledge children will, theoretically, pass from a home-bound, constraining and ego-centric orientation to an orientation with advanced and sophisticated authority figures and a (co-operative) sociocentredness. Primarily, the study searches for development of knowledge of the authority of the teacher and peer; at what age and with what type of awareness the authority recognition takes place. In applying a contextual perspective, the classroom behaviours between children themselves and children and their teachers are observed. From the patterns of interaction and developmental recognition one can explore what may loosely be called patterns of social understanding. These patterns include how behaviour may facilitate cognitive recognition (Law of Conscious Realisation), the strictness and confines of the environment (in allowing certain ritualised or habitualised behaviours) and how the child's recognition is shaped by this environment. Subsidiary, but theoretically important to the study, are: (1) the type of authority acknowledged by the child in (a) recognition of constraining and co-operative *deep* structures, and (b) *surface* structure of the authority of teacher (if it follows the intellectual and instrumental qualities noted by Musgrove and Taylor, 1969) and peer group (a relatively unexplored topic); (2) if sex differences play any part in this developing knowledge of authority; (3) how all of the above may be reflective of the child's developing competence (for almost all of us accept the school's role as facilitator of development, but rarely question its confining and inhibiting role except in studies of self-fulfilling prophecy); (4) the role of the school as a social/moral/political agency.

METHODOLOGY

Furth (1978) points out that one of the most important perspectives in Piaget's research and writings is the bridge between the (philosophical and other) gaps of action and knowledge. Piaget has been one of the few researchers to discuss behaviour's link to knowledge: that all behaviour is governed by knowledge and that most theoretical knowledge is derived developmentally from action knowledge. Damon (1977) has similarly noted that a child's social development can be understood through analysing 'active and verbal' manifestations in relation to the social knowledge of others. To come to this understanding, Damon states, there is no single technique. One must search for organising principles of development. The above comments place the study within the developmental camp. But one must maintain an awareness (and use) of Wohlwill's (1973) critique that most developmental psychology assumes age to be the major variable and does not allow or account for situation or context.

Research on the school and schooling should embody aspects of development in the actual classroom context. Simply by noting the potential of a primary-school-based study, a design for a more comprehensive study may be evolved. One of the few studies that has noted behavioural and cognitive dimensions of development (of the primary school child) is by Furth and Wachs (1974). They adapt an elementary school curriculum to promote (behavioural) manipulative, physical and social skills in advance of the children's cognitive development. The study by Bennett (1976) and his colleagues attempts to focus on the effect of teaching styles upon primary pupils' learning: an ambitious piece of research which defines teachers' attitudes and thoughts about teaching, observes children's classroom behaviours and tests intellectual performance. Bennett's research contains numerous methodological pitfalls and inconsistencies (as noted in the many critical review articles written after its publication). Recent reanalysis has considerably altered the original findings.

The research cited above helps to focus on criteria necessary for an adequate study of the primary school. Primarily, the school presents itself as an arena for behaviour, whether it is of the gross physical action, subtle gesture, or verbal interchange. Behaviours can be observed, tallied and compared between individuals and across age-groups. Insight can be drawn from the simplest of the gross behavioural movements to show how (1) particular movements facilitate cognitive and social advancement (as in Furth and Wachs, 1974; an exploration of pre-operative schemes), and (2) particular teacher behaviours or teaching styles affect pupil performance (as in the studies of the moulding of divergent thinking abilities by Haddon and Lytton, 1969; reflective teacher effecting a reflective change in pupils by Yando and Kagan, 1968; and Bennett, 1976). From research on gross behavioural movement, studies of more refined communicative behaviours have explored ego-centric and social communication (see Rubin, 1973) and teacher control of knowledge/pupil competence (in questioning and information transmission style, as in Rosen, 1972, and Barnes, 1976). Behaviours maintain an important role in promoting intellectual development and in setting the limits of both social and intellectual interactions.

Children's knowledge of their environment should be qualified by development of awareness of the surrounding environment. In exploring children's knowledge one can seek principles of organisation (as described by Damon, 1977), e.g. dimensions of authority, socio-centricity, surface and deep structures. By comparing children's knowledge with their behavioural actions and context, one derives *grounded* (from Glaser and Strauss, 1967) insights into develop-ment. Knowledge is qualified in conjunction with the context in which it took place. Only in observing, recording and noting the environ-ment, behaviour and knowledge can one adequately evolve a theory capable of describing fully a social and developmental psychology of the primary school.

Observation

The observation and recording of behaviour has been an area of study in the social and biological sciences for some time. Observers (partici-pant and non-participant) argue that their task is to record and analyse behaviour in a natural, normative and systematic manner. The sheer range in type and focus of observation causes methodological and ideological conflict. Observational studies appear to have two ex-tremes or poles: ethology and the observational schedule. Ethological studies attempt to record all behaviours of an animal in a natural context. From the recordings, patterns of behaviour which are re-peated in particular contexts are derived. Ethology requires a non-inferential and non-participant recorder who notes the physical actions of the animal being studied. From the recorded patterns, comparisons can be made in development (cf. Lawick-Goodall, 1976) between environments and species. Recently researchers such as Blurton Jones (1976) and Smith (1974) have applied ethological methods to the study of children.

In contrast to the naturalistic style of ethology is the more normative style of observation schedules. A schedule is designed to note the occurrence and frequency of particularly (operationally) defined be-haviours. The school, especially the American elementary school, has been the main focus of observation schedules. Methods using a schedule have been developed and used through the twentieth cen-tury. As Delamont (1976) and her colleagues (Chanan and Delamont, 1975; Stubbs, 1976) point out, the school-based application increased greatly after the Second World War. Delamont places schedule origin, development and methodology within the 'liberal' and 'democratic' context of American social psychology. Models of democracy were sought in the school in early studies of the dominative and integrative behaviours of teachers (Anderson and Brewer, 1946) and refined in the Flanders Teacher–Pupil Interaction schedule (FIAC). A review and analysis of the American schedules (mainly based on FIAC or variations) is presented by Amidon and Hough (1967) and further development of schedules and methods is included in an anthology of observation schedules, *Mirrors for Behaviour* (Simon and Boyer, 1970). Delamont states that the main direction of the American research was to note that greater indirect and less dominative forms of teacher (control) behaviour would create a more favourable attitude for pupil learning and pupils would in fact learn more. While the first effect is generally accepted, the second is highly debatable (see Rosenshine and Furst, 1973).

The use of an observation schedule does require a host of methodological precautions. Minimally, one must account for the validity of the schedule in the origin of categories, definitions of behaviour and accountability as precise units (face, content and structure validities). Validity questions the truthfulness and real appearance of behaviours that are observed. Do the categories listed on an observation schedule actually occur and is their definition correct? What is the limited degree of inference and associated reliability between observers and over-time? Reliability ensures that we see the same thing at the same time. It also ensures that what happens in a specific context is likely to happen again in the same context (for a further discussion see Kerlinger, 1973). An adequate observation schedule must take into account real behaviours in real situations. It is invariably grounded in preliminary ethological observations. Associated with problems concerning use of a schedule is the type of sampling used, for example, anecdotal diary, checklist, frequency of events and time frequencies (see Cartwright and Cartwright, 1974; Rosenshine and Furst, 1973). Appropriateness of sampling is vitally important for the information extracted from observations and its generalisability. A frequency count of teacher behaviours totals the number of times that a behaviour takes place. Frequency counts provide a general description of teaching style. They do not account for the action–reaction (of a timed sample) and development of behaviour in a pupil–teacher interchange. Timed samples count the same behaviours but record the behaviours in a timed sequence, noting which behaviours follow one another. The above qualification of use should not be construed in terms of one sampling method being better than another, but as a clarification of choice for appropriate use.

The contrast or polarity of observation method (ethological or schedule) is not as absolute as some writers would have us believe. The background to many observational studies combines elements of both ethological and schedule methods. In fact, any adequate schedule must have an ethological basis (whether a schedule is a direct development from ethology or relies upon ethological validity; see Hutt and Hutt, 1970, for further discussion). Alternatively, in a number of cases ethologists have found it more useful to develop a schedule from their earlier systematic observations. Blurton Jones has developed a schedule of rough-and-tumble play from his ethological observations.

Further, in using any observational method, one must still maintain an awareness of, or check on, the fuller context and history of the situation (as discussed in Adelman and Walker, 1975). Greater awareness is often gained from the combined use of a schedule with ethological follow-up and interviews on incidents that are usual. It must be remembered that schedules must be used only in the context for which they were developed. Otherwise, valid conclusions could not be drawn from application of a schedule: FIAC and Anderson's schedules, for instance, were developed for American elementary schools and should not be used in secondary schools.

Verbal Awareness
Recording and noting children's knowledge (intellectual, moral, social) also has a long history. There are multiple methodologies to elicit content and structure. Youniss (1978) has pointed out a shift in earlier psychological research from the broad term socialisation to a more tightly defined cognition and exploration into its associated processes of today. Cognition is an 'enabling device which mediates social development'; a basis for assigning meaning and a basis for behaviour. In any cognitive study the search is for ongoing and developing organising principles. According to Damon (1977), organising principles are stable, are used consistently and appear/reappear spontaneously. Techniques to elicit knowledge and organising principles (in the form of surface and deep structures, in Damon's terminology) must demonstrate when knowledge meets the consistency, stability and appearance criteria. The eliciting must allow for the minimum of inference by adults (researchers). Damon further cites criteria for an adequate methodology. Research methods should be simple yet sophisticated enough to elicit meaningful information. Any structural interpretation of information elicited should serve as the basis for (1) conclusions as to stage of knowledge, (2) the sequence or order of stages and (3) decalage, the movement within and between stages. The cognitive information/methodology being written about will necessarily rely upon interview procedures/techniques which can supplement and expand behavioural knowledge. Standard questionnaire procedures with particular (methodologically pre-ordained) response categories are not appropriate for cognitive/structural information. Piaget used clinical methods for exploring a child's knowledge by (1) relating a story or action to the child, (2) asking for a judgement to be made or information to be provided and (3) probing as to origin and extent of the child's answer. The clinical method has been used most frequently as the model for cognitive studies. Briefly, the clinical method allows the child to provide information in her/his own terms. Probing will draw out the complexity of understanding, insights into origin/development and limits of generalisability. Damon has noted that this

method maintains a balance of structure *v.* aimlessness. It is flexible but permits comparison, and the child plays an active role.

Social class, background and age of children interviewed also provide limitations to the cognitive study. Researchers have found very limited effects of social class between children of a similar age-grouping in studies of cognitive abilities. But the role of environment and experience does appear to facilitate or inhibit (to a limited extent) cognitive growth (see Cole and Scribner, 1974; Bruner, 1974). The child's development can be encouraged in stimulating surroundings and depressed by lack of stimulation. Also the type of activities available to the child in and around the home will set early guides to experience. The home of a Mexican peasant potter will be more oriented to physical manipulation of items than one operated by advanced push buttons in a high-technology society.

In searching for knowledge and organising principles it is important to collect information across an age-range. Age development is important not only for the greater amount of information to which the child has access. The methods by which the child adapts information develop (for example, from the action of pre-operations to the reflections of concrete operations). The insights that can be drawn from information by new groupings and classifications extend the range and depth of understanding. Techniques that most adequately describe development through childhood (and beyond) are discussed by Wohlwill (1973). He points to the two basic methods of longitudinal and cross-sectional studies. Longitudinal research has the advantage of following individual development over time and thus connections between early behaviours and later life can be made. But Wohlwill also notes disadvantages, such as the following: the researcher must prepare the study adequately – he cannot go back later and collect missing information; the study is very time-consuming over years; there can be large-scale subject attrition over the years; and the researcher is unable to provide test-retest measures. Cross-sectional research, on the other hand, only uses samples of subjects. It is not statistically efficient (as is longitudinal research). It is not directly comparable between subjects and over time, but provides for direction and style of change. Aspects of the two methods can be used separately or combined, depending on the amount, type, complexity and generalisability of the information sought. Quantification of information elicited for research and display purposes inevitably involves a contradiction. The information sought in cognitive interviews is qualitative. The interviews seek change from one mode of thought to another. Traditional measures of validity and reliability must be accounted for as well; these measures seek to quantify the results.

Methods described here are qualitative. The study described below seeks to plot the development of knowledge and structure due to maturational, experiential and constructive limitations. The study does not seek individual differences between children.

THE STUDY

I have now provided a broad focus of the methodologies relevant to the study of the 'behavioural interactions and verbal knowledge of authority patterns between children, their teachers and their peers' discussed at the start of this chapter. As previously noted, the study searches for type and knowledge of authority and the effects of behavioural and verbal interactions in the primary school classroom. It focuses on the general development of school authority using three distinct methodologies, which investigate (1) cognitive knowledge of authority, (2) behavioural interactions in schools and (3) a general perceptual study relating home and school effects of development.

(1) Knowledge of Social Authority (in the Classroom)

The classroom role of the teacher has previously been described (Chapter 3) in terms of the intellectual and instrumental nature of the position. This individual appears to maintain an authority based on advanced knowledge and the ability to manipulate or control the behaviours of children. While the teacher's role has been so described there has been no verification that children actually see and acknowledge the teacher as such (most child–teacher research is based upon an affective liking of, or identification with, the teacher). This first part of the study explores the child's knowledge of the teacher. Similarly, it explores children's authority concept among classroom peers – the group and authority noted for its co-operative or communal structure.

In developing an instrument and procedure that could elicit information about children's knowledge of school authority, I had to bear in mind the necessary age-groupings and intellectual interest and authority constraints. To cover the range and type of development a cross-sectional design was chosen, covering the age-range from reception class (4 years) to the upper limit of the primary school (11 years). It has been found that young children are highly distractable and have difficulty in providing answers to written or story questions (as in Magowan and Lee, 1970); this technique can and has only been effective with older children (adolescent and beyond, as in Kohlberg, 1976; Loevinger, 1976). The method chosen to elicit knowledge was adapted from projective techniques. These, linked with clinical interviewing procedures, elicit cognitive and affective factors in a neutral and unstructured manner (see Anastasi, 1961; Bull, 1969). Individual pictures depicting human figures of an adult (male, female) in a neutral (i.e. non-activity) home situation, an adult (female, male) in a neutral classroom setting, children talking and children playing were drawn for displaying to the children (see Appendix 1). Use of the pictures overcame the testing limitations of 4-year-olds and provided a common focus for all the children interviewed.

Questions centred on figures in the pictures – who they might be. If the child identified (authority) figures of parents, teachers, or peers, a thorough exploration of the type and structure of that knowledge was pursued. Once children from all age-groups had been interviewed, an analysis for type and structure of authority was made. The children's answers were then retrospectively analysed for their acknowledgement of the authority types known by all of the children. The analysis provided self-generated categories of authority and a sequence of development. Apart from providing information about school authority, the samples of children chosen enabled comparisons to be made between girls and boys, and children from working- and middle-class backgrounds. The study was also conducted in the United States to provide a cross-cultural comparison. As a critical aside to this procedure, the reader will properly question the role/authority of the adult interviewer in relation to the answering child. I can only note that lengthy familiarisation procedures were carried out before the interviews. As the interviews took place in schools, the interviewer spent many days in individual classrooms as a non-participant observer. Interviews were conducted with single children outside the classroom and started with the child drawing a picture for the interviewer and explaining its content.

(2) Behavioural Actions and Interactions in the Classroom

As previously noted, actions (in behavioural and verbal forms) develop over time, are expressive of particular relationships and are linked with conscious realisation. When observing in a primary school classroom, one quickly becomes aware of three types of action which observation methods must be sophisticated enough to detect and record. The actions may be defined as general teacher behaviour, child behaviour and teacher–child interactions. After preliminary observations had been made, a search for an observation methodology (from the range of ethological to schedule-based studies) was carried out. Three observational schedules were chosen as appropriate to record: Teacher Behaviour (Anderson and Brewer, 1946); Child Behaviour (Anderson and Brewer, 1946); and Teacher–Pupil Interaction (FIAC) (see Appendix 2). The schedules were used in a pilot study to test for appropriateness, validity, flexibility and sampling procedures. Teacher and Child Behaviour schedules were used in their original form. It was thought that an additional category of 'deviance' was a necessary addition to the FIAC (for children often deliberately or spontaneously disobeyed teacher directions, an important focus of classroom interaction).

The sampling procedure was adapted so that the schedules would provide insight into the 'style' of the classroom, that is, characteristic modes of behaviour that did not require the minute-by-minute recording of action, reaction and interaction. To provide for the style, a frequency count of appropriate behaviours was made per schedule. Counts were made during three five-minute observation sessions, spread over morning and afternoon on several days. Instead of using the Child Behaviour schedule to observe individual children, the classrooms were mapped (broken down) into area groupings in which five or six children normally worked. In each observation session one Teacher Behaviour, one Teacher–Pupil Interaction and three Child Behaviour schedules were used. Once the validity of the schedules had been chosen and checked, observations were also checked for reliability by correlations with a colleague. Seven classrooms per school (one classroom per year-grouping) from three schools were selected for observation. The frequency counts per schedule provided for comparisons:

(1) within classrooms to insure for style;
(2) between schools, as schools were selected from working- and middle-class housing areas in north London;
(3) of development of actions over the years of primary schooling.

Before observations were made there was a familiarisation period of several days per classroom. The cross-cultural comparison, using the same observational procedures, was made in two elementary schools in the United States.

As the classrooms observed were the same as those used for the interviews already described (in fact the observation and interviews were carried out simultaneously), a combination of these two parts of the study provides a behaviour–knowledge comparison.

(3) Perceptual Understanding of School Authority

The first two parts of the study noted cognitive elements of school authority (of teacher and peer) and its relation to general classroom behaviours. But the results offer limited insight into the generation of this knowledge outside the immediate classroom environment. A further interview study was conducted along the lines of the 'Knowledge of Social Authority' (e.g. using a cognitive/projective technique of the pictures and probing of information elicited from the children). But the perceptual understanding study sought particular comparisons between the authority figures generated by the children. Were teachers seen as similar to parents? Did parents have responsibilities similar to those of teachers? Where did the concept of leadership originate? Familiarisation and questioning procedures were similar to those used in the first part of the study with the exception that parents, teachers and leaders were identified for the children before the interviews took place. Analysis of the interview data was based upon categories generated by the children's responses and retrospectively coded. Additionally, categories of types of authority were adopted from Wood (1968). Children interviewed ranged in age from 4½ to 11½ years and were selected by random procedures from two schools in north London. Comparisons were made between boys and girls, and working and middle classes.

The results of the three parts of the study are described and displayed in Chapter 5. Their educational implications are taken up in Chapter 6.

The Three-Part Study and its Results

The study described here draws upon the range of methodologies discussed in Chapter 4. Separately, the three parts of the study explore the child's developing recognition of figures of authority outside the home and schemes or processes by which this information is made available and adapted by the child. By bringing together the separate parts, a picture of the child's entry into the social world of the school is built up. Underlying the entry into the social world beyond the home (and the basic premise of this book) are the interpersonal relationships of the child; and underlying these relationships are relations of power/ authority (see Chapter 2). Classically, one can portray the child's school social development as having its roots in the family home with its adult-oriented power (authority of parents, relatives) relations. Introduction to schools extends adult-oriented authority relations (teacher, headmaster) while introducing the child into organisations and bureaucracies, and providing for multiple peer relationships (allowing for possible co-operative and/or constraining authority relations). How the child adapts to the school situation is explored here. From interviews and observation the content of children's school authority knowledge and the process of gaining that knowledge are illuminated.

KNOWLEDGE OF SOCIAL AUTHORITY (IN THE CLASSROOM)

Before this part of the study could proceed, I first needed to know what the child understood by authority. The first set of interviews sought to establish the types of authority with which the child was familiar. For this set of interviews, authority was broadly defined as a power relationship between people. The interviews were sensitive to the fact that power could (1) be presented as one individual controlling another (as in a *hierarchy*) (2) be shared among equals (*mutuality*). The interviews focused on key types of individuals in the child's life. One can assume from relationships in the home that most children would have some understanding of parental power. But did children actually acknowledge their subservient role? What relationship did children have with their teacher? And was there any mutuality of power expressed among peers? Or was leadership a replication of the parental relationship (similar to that in the primal horde described by Freud)?

The interviews were conducted by showing a child, individually, each of the pictures that were drawn for the study. The child was first encouraged to identify individuals in the pictures; whether there were boys or girls, men or women, and who these people might be. Once the child had identified individuals as parents, teachers, friends, and so on, a discussion of their responsibilities and duties ensued. This probing of the children's statements is known as the clinical method (developed to a great extent by Piaget). In all, 120 children were interviewed (60 boys and 60 girls). The children's ages ranged from 4 years 8 months to 11 years 5 months. The children were selected from three schools in north London, chosen to provide one school from a predominantly working-class housing area, one school from a middle-class area and one from a mixed area. All the interviews were tape-recorded for ease of analysis.

After all the interviews had been carried out, an analysis of the tapes was made. Across the age-range the children showed a varied and sophisticated understanding of authority and the people who wield it. Somewhat surprisingly, many of the younger children did not identify parents in the pictures. Without the identification of a mother or father, concepts of parental authority could not be explored. Overall, the interviews revealed: (1) a broad concept of parental authority; (2) two distinct concepts of teacher; (3) two not-so-distinct concepts of leader. The concepts actually developed during their years of primary schooling. Concepts of teacher were labelled, *Teacher as Teacher* and *Teacher as Disciplinarian*. Peer authorities were labelled as *Leadership* and *Submissiveness to Peer Leadership*. The labels may best be explained citing examples of the recorded interviews.

Of the youngest children who identified a parent in the pictures, most asserted that parental authority was hierarchical. They showed an awareness of parents usually 'telling' or 'asking' the children to do something. When questioned as to how they knew the figure in the picture was a mummy or daddy, most answered 'Because I know' or 'He is the biggest', or simply provided a description of the picture, such as 'They are talking'. Thomas (4 years 8 months) gave a clear indication of his knowledge of parental authority by describing his mother as saying 'Play close by . . . and telling them'. Slightly older children specified parental directions with an overlay of moral or value sentiment. Phillip (5:11) said that the mother was 'telling them not to misbehave'. Janet (9:11) said that the mother was having a discussion; she told the boy to 'shut the door' and that a boy 'might have done something naughty'. The interviews did not explore further type and extent of assertion of parental authority. They did reveal that there were size/power and behavioural/moral controls characteristic of parental authority which were recognised by all age-groups. For ease of labelling, this parental power/authority was simply termed *Parental*.

Understanding of the teacher was quite different from that of parents. All the children interviewed were shown pictures of classrooms. Children and some classroom activity were recognised in the pictures, but the youngest children had no concept of teacher. Boys and girls were seen as working or writing, but teachers had nothing to do. Often the adult in the classroom pictures was identified as a mother or father by the youngest children. However, children by the end of their first year in school (end of reception year) and in the start of their second year at school (first-year infant) had a clear idea of teacher role and responsibility. Thomas (4:9) said: 'Teachers tell them how to write . . . and how to do it.' Whereas Bobby (4:8) saw children 'writing in a classroom', but could say nothing about teachers. Phillip (5:11) identified a teacher (in the picture) by the classroom context and 'telling them what they are going to write'. Joanne (5:11) described the children's actions (writing) and said: 'The teacher was telling them what to do, such as get your history books out.' Carey (5:12) simply knew it was a teacher in the drawing 'because she learns people things'. The earliest recognition of the teacher was that of an individual closely connected with numbers, letters, writing and classroom materials. The classroom teaching responsibilities of teacher provided the *Teacher as Teacher* label.

The *Teacher as Teacher* understanding was maintained by virtually all the older children. Additionally, their understanding expanded to recognise that teachers also controlled their behaviour. Andrew (8:5), after identifying a teacher in the picture, said he knew it was a teacher 'because teachers move from the desk and children are not allowed; they are told not to move . . . Teachers teach sums and ask questions . . .' Robert (11:4) thought the children were doing exams, and said: 'If I were a teacher and saw one was looking at another, I would say that they are copying. I would take a mark off.' So, while the general instructional role of the teacher became more sophisticated with school experience (e.g. Beverley, 11:2, 'I'd tell them to get their books out and what is on the timetable and . . . um . . . give them some work which they would write in their exercise books'), a growing realisation of control over behaviour also took place (e.g. cheating, talking aloud, moving around without permission). The second teacher role was labelled *Teacher as Disciplinarian*.

Leadership was a difficult topic to approach with young children. The younger children most often named anyone bigger as a 'mummy' or 'daddy' or, more simply, an adult who gave directions. They had not heard of or used the word 'leader'. Specific prompting, such as 'Is there a leader in the picture?', brought the following responses:

Phillip (5:11):   Yes
Interviewer: Which one?
Phillip: (Points)
Interviewer: How can you tell that that one is a leader?
Phillip: Because he's bigger.

A leader for Phillip was someone who was different. Andrew (8:5) said that the leader was 'giving directions' and 'telling them which way to go'. The oldest children understood that the leader's responsibility was to direct others. Beverley (11:2) also said that leaders 'look after' their group, and the children's/followers' responsibility was 'to follow the leader'. Recognition of leader had two aspects: (1) the forthright assertion of hierarchical power and direction, labelled *Leadership*; and (2) a reciprocal understanding that the followers' responsibility was to carry out the leader's dictations, labelled *Submissiveness*. Leader authority was very similar to parental authority.

After the five types of authority recognised by the children had been labelled, all interviews were analysed for their presence. Table 5.1 shows a constant level of authority acknowledgement in *Parent*. A substantial number of children in all the age-groups recognised authority in the role of parent. There are developing trends from youngest to oldest in all the further authorities. Noticeably, there is a dramatic jump from 16·7 to 94·4 per cent in *Teacher as Teacher* between the first two year groups. Very few children had any recognition of teacher in the reception class. But nearly all the infant-aged schoolchildren recognised the teacher's intellectual role. The table supports earlier research on the role of the teacher (Morrison and McIntyre, 1969; Musgrove and Taylor, 1969) in that there are two perceived classroom roles for the teacher. The recognition appears strongly age-related. Leadership is also age-related. Curiously, the authority described in leadership is similar to the hierarchical principles of adult-oriented

Table 5.1   *Authority Acknowledgement by Percentage of Age-Grouping*

Age	Parent	Teacher as Teacher	Peer Leader	Teacher as Disciplinarian	Peer Submissiveness
4:6–5:5	50·0	16·7	8·3	0·6	8·3
5:6–6:5	72·2	94·4	16·7	22·2	0·0
6:6–7:5	66·7	83·3	22·2	33·3	0·0
7:6–8:5	52·9	93·8	50·0	43·8	12·5
8:6–9:5	80·0	85·0	75·0	60·0	30·0
9:6–10:5	77·8	94·7	89·5	52·6	68·4
10:5–11:6	76·5	94·1	100·0	64·7	100·0

authority. There is one above who commands while others follow. There are no mutual or co-operative aspects to the authority of the leader. The ability to command appears to be based on either the position of leader or the sheer physical size of the individual.

Table 5.2 shows average age per progressive authority recognition using a scalogram analysis. This analysis shows a step-wise progression of the children's recognition of school authorities, and the order in which the children's recognition took place.

Upon obtaining the strong developmental trends above, the author made comparisons within the data to detect sex and social class differences. Differences due to sex or social class were not found to be significant. The lack of significant difference indicated the underlying cognitive nature of the data. Knowledge and recognition of the school authority figures was gained through experience. And all the children interviewed had nearly the same school experience.

A more interesting comparison is shown in the cross-cultural data. The same study/procedures were replicated in Detroit, Michigan, USA. Detroit was selected for its similarity in range of social class and industrialisation to the north London area where the original study was set. Seventy children were selected from two schools on the outskirts of Detroit. Results from the interviews showed all the same age developmental trends in recognition of school authority. There were no significant sex or social class differences. When the averaged age per recognition was obtained and compared with the English sample (shown in Table 5.2), consistent developmental differences were found.

Table 5.3 shows that, on average, the American children were 6 months older when they recognised teacher and leader authorities. Two simplistic but significant points may be drawn from this comparison. First, Detroit children, on average, started school later than English children; (5+ years as compared with 4¾ years, in many cases). Second, what is often referred to as age development is really

Table 5.2 *Averaged Age per Recognition (Scalogram Analysis)*

Average Age	Parent	Teacher as Teacher	Peer Leader	Teacher as Disciplinarian	Peer Submissiveness
5:1	+				
6:2	+	+			
7:4	+	+	+		
8:7	+	+	+	+	
10:2	+	+	+	+	+

Note
Scalogram analysis (Green, 1956 method): reproducibility 0·928, index of consistency, 0·53.

Table 5.3   *Comparison of Averaged Age per Recognition of School Authority*

	Parent	Teacher as Teacher	Peer Leader	Teacher as Disciplinarian	Peer Submissiveness
English	5:1	6:2	7:4	8:7	10:2
American	5:7	6:9	8:0	9:0	10:8
Difference	6	7	8	3	6

Average of all age differences: 6 months.

synonymous with the *experiences* necessary to generate social-cognitive knowledge. It is not a simple matter of maturity which promotes development, but the complex interaction between the child and experiences in the environment. Overall, the developmental progress in authority recognition shows a developing sophistication of knowledge, qualified by the experiences of childhood.

BEHAVIOURAL ACTIONS AND INTERACTIONS IN THE CLASSROOM

The previous study noted a developing sophistication in authority concepts characteristic of the primary school. The interviews and interview technique found this knowledge to be deeply rooted in the day-to-day school and classroom activities of the child. Very often the child spoke of (or recalled) the teacher's role in terms of what his or her teachers actually said or the directions that they gave. The selected observation schedules (described in Chapter 4) were used to document the style of teacher and pupil classroom behaviours and interactions. Quantification of the frequency counts on each schedule could be used for the following comparisons: (1) within classrooms to note characteristic behaviours of children and teachers; (2) between schools to check for social class/environment differences, for schools were chosen from working and middle class areas; (3) for development of children over the schooling years; (4) with elementary schools in Detroit for a cross-cultural comparison.

Comparisons and associations were made within each classroom. In order to draw any valid conclusions about the 'style' of individual teachers, a significant association had to be found between the three administrations per schedule in each classroom (remembering that minimally one administration was undertaken in the morning and one in the afternoon). All associations and reliability checks (from the twenty-one classrooms) were averaged and found to be significantly associated (see Appendix 3). The singular conclusion that may be drawn is that teacher and child behavioural interactions in each classroom observed were roughly similar throughout the day. Classroom style (democratic, dogmatic, deterministic, or whatever) is consistent through most activities.

Comparisons between schools provided a test of differences of the working- and middle-class communities that feed the schools. Although there were over fifty categories compared, in only four categories were differences statistically significant. Appendix 4 shows the significant differences between the behaviours of pupils and teachers of the working- and middle-class schools.

All four of the categories showed that teachers of working-class children and working-class children themselves, exhibited a higher frequency of interactions than middle-class children. The greater number of interactions may have multiple causes. More teacher–pupil interaction has been interpreted as evidence of greater dependence on the teacher by working-class children, with middle-class children being more self-confident and competent. The reader's attention will be drawn to the point that the behaviours of teachers of working-class children coincide with those children's behaviours. With the greater amount of pupil activity, there is a greater amount of teacher determining behaviours. The coincidence provides a non-causal chicken-and-egg or self-fulfilling prophecy argument as to which precedes the other. Further longitudinal research will be needed to explore precisely specific development of these behaviours.

After the initial comparisons were carried out, the frequencies per category were plotted on graphs and tested for age developmental differences. Table 5.4 provides a general list of increases and decreases in frequency of behaviours over the primary school years. In each category, if there were few incidents of that behaviour (such as 'asks questions') in the reception class, but a growing frequency through the infant and junior classes, this was labelled *Increase*. A *Decrease* was the opposite, that is, high frequency in the reception class leading to fewer incidents in the infant and junior classes.

Table 5.4 provides a general picture of the reception teacher being kind, sympathetic and very involved with the pupils. As children progressed through their school years, teachers became more formal. They asked specific questions and directed children to particular activities. Interactions took place in relation to the children's work and their classroom misbehaviour (or lack of classroom work). Children were quick to pick up on the less loving, more formal teacher. They asked specific questions and avoided general chat to the teacher. On the other hand, children became more acutely aware of their peers. Fruitful verbal and physical contacts took place among themselves.

Figures 5.1(a) and 5.1(b) are characteristic of a particular classroom peer interaction, that of deviance. Classroom deviance was defined as the verbal and physical behaviours of a child made specifically against a teacher's wishes. The deviance usually took place with another child.

Table 5.4   *Significant Increases/Decreases in Frequency per Category in Years of Primary Schooling*

Schedule	Category	Increase/Decrease
Flanders	Asks Questions	Increase
	Directed Activity	Increase
	Deviance	Increase
	Pupil Questions	Increase
	Corrective Feedback	Increase
	Accepting Telling	Decrease
	Praising	Decrease
	Pupil Talking to Teacher	Decrease
Teacher Behaviour	Warning	Increase
	Helping	Decrease
	Approval	Decrease
	Joint Activity	Decrease
	Sympathy	Decrease
Child Behaviour	Deviance	Increase
	Child Domination	Increase
	Helping Other Children	Increase
	Response to Telling Experiences	Increase

Most obvious deviant behaviours were talking out of turn, wise-cracking, and throwing or dropping some object (pencil, eraser, chalk, book, etc.) Deviant acts also appeared to take the form of a ritualised (gestural) attempt to communicate with another child. (Perhaps an interpretation of *some* school deviance problems would be to see these actions as a frustrated attempt to talk to another child which, in the past, has been stopped by a teacher. As a result of being told not to talk, the individual child – with good social communication skills – has been forced to develop this *non-verbal communication* with peers.) Interestingly, deviance occurred on the classroom scene at roughly the

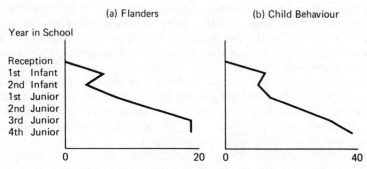

Figure 5.1   *Incidents of classroom deviance.*

age that Piaget noted that the child's speech becomes most fully socio-centric, that is, about age 8. Teacher disciplinary behaviours such as warning and disapproving followed a similar progression to that on the graphs of deviance, showing a major jump in frequency of occurrence at the start of the junior school level, and thus leaving the chicken-and-egg controversy unresolved.

A behaviour that was not specifically accounted for among peers was 'group work' or co-operative activities. The schedules were sufficiently sophisticated to note these behaviours among children. The older children spontaneously helped one another and responded to one another. Most of the seating arrangements found children grouped around tables. The children worked and occasionally chatted to one another in a limited space. But they rarely discussed their work with each other. All corrections and feedback were undertaken by the teacher. The children were each working for their individual development. Given the individual nature of classroom work, one might say that the children were co-acting (doing the same thing in the same place as others) but not co-operating. Group work was, thus, very curiously defined.

In reviewing all the categories of teacher behaviour, it is both vital and interesting to note that two categories increased with age-groups taught. Many other categories held constant, but there was a noticeable increase in teachers giving warnings/directions and providing specific corrective feedback. Teachers continually picked up on and extended pupil ideas, asked questions, gave schoolwork directions, and handed out materials to pupils from the reception class to the oldest juniors.

Thus teachers' behaviour through the years of primary education was contradictory. Many of the main behaviours remained constantly in use. The initial caring and sympathetic personality evolved to a more rigid individual with specific expectations about classroom behaviour and educational control. It was the caring, loving and feeling teacher who eased the young child into the school situation and made the transition from the home most enjoyable by providing many home comforts. Behaviours of the more formalised teacher may be accounted for by the need to prepare older pupils for secondary schooling, as well as providing a more varied (less integrated) school curriculum with ensuing timing and timetable constraints. The constraints of specialised curriculum and a formalised teaching approach combine with the developing social perspectives of pupils in formulating the dual nature of the teacher's role and perceived responsibilities as Teacher and Disciplinarian. Just how these coincide with the previous interviews will be discussed later.

Teacher and pupil behaviour and interactions were also compared (using similar measures and procedures) with the schools in Detroit,

Michigan (used in the interview study). The results of this observation study virtually replicated the previous results. Briefly: the separate administrations of schedules per classroom were highly associated (averaged $p < 0.01$); the few significant social class differences were in pupils' response to teacher (Flanders, $p < 0.02$, MC > WC) and responding to other pupils' talk (Child Behaviour, $p < 0.01$, WC > MC). Middle-class children appeared more teacher-oriented and working-class children were more peer-oriented. (It should also be re-emphasised here that while over fifty categories were compared, only the two just mentioned were significantly different.) Behaviours that increased or decreased with the year in school are displayed in Table 5.5.

Developmental findings showed: (1) the teacher became less child-centred and more involved in teaching specific lessons; (2) older children made progressively greater use of teacher knowledge; (3) by the fourth year in school, children's attention became split between teacher and peers.

Tests for significance of association with the London behavioural study were conducted between classrooms by year of school experience. (Averaged levels of significance of association per schedule were: Flanders $p < 0.01$, Teacher Behaviour $p < 0.01$ and Child Behaviour $p < 0.05$.) The significant level of association in all the comparisons demonstrated a basic developmental similarity between the Detroit and London schools. Patterns of behavioural action and interaction were nearly the same, as defined by year of school experience.

Table 5.5   *Significant Increases/Decreases in Frequency per Category in Years of Primary Schooling (Detroit)*

Schedule	Category	Increase/Decrease
Flanders	Answer Pupil Questions	Increase
	Corrective Feedback	Increase
	Deviance	Increase
Teacher Behaviour	Accept Teaching	Decrease
	Praise	Decrease
	Warm	Increase
	Help Redefine	Decrease
	Approval	Decrease
Child Behaviour	Deviance	Increase
	Nervous Habits	Increase
	Answer in Response	Increase
	Answer Spontaneously	Decrease

INTEGRATION OF KNOWLEDGE AND BEHAVIOURAL STUDIES

The results that have thus far been presented may not strike the reader as startling or unique. In fact, many of them may appear as commonplace. Children's knowledge of teacher and peer authority shows an underlying basis of constraint, or recognition of a hierarchical authority. Knowledge develops with experience over time. Teacher and pupil behaviours and interactions develop, as the child progresses through the primary school, from child-centred to knowledge-oriented, teacher-centred classrooms. Children play a major role in this development. They acknowledge (and make use of) the redefined teacher role. They seek alternative attentions in the classroom through peer interaction. The two studies already described help to qualify (and quantify) the above points.

Additionally, a combination of the knowledge and behaviour studies provides theoretical and practical insights to problems focused upon in the earlier chapters. The combination of the studies illuminates two schemes of social development. Both behaviour and knowledge have been explored in the specific context in which they naturally occur. The studies place major responsibility on both school and teacher for the setting of the context. Theoretically, the combination of studies illuminates two schemes of social development. Practically, the range of behaviours limited to the classroom sets the basis for the development of school and social knowledge. The combination provides insights into how and why social context provides for development.

Figure 5.2 is derived from a combination of the two major parts of the study. Surveying teacher behaviours and children's knowledge and understanding of the teacher, one may notice the two specific *schemes* of development. First, behavioural interactions between child and teacher were quite evident during the first year in school (and remained so throughout school). The interactions are noted by the 'o's in the first column in Figure 5.2. While the behavioural actions were constant through all the school years, the child's acknowledgement of these actions did not take place until the second year in school (see the '+'s in the *Teacher as Teacher* column in years 1 and 2). Recognition/acknowledgement/understanding of the instructional role of the teacher was derived through constant repetition (ritualisation) of pupil and teacher behaviours in the first year at school. The scheme by which repeated behavioural actions are eventually acknowledged by the child is pre-operational. The scheme of repeated action leading eventually to realisation is an example of Piaget's Law of Conscious Realisation and the type of action–learning sequence characteristic of conservation. What is demonstrated here is that school and social knowledge is adapted in the same way as logical-mathematical know-

Year in school	Recognition of:			
	Teacher as Teacher	Teacher as Disciplinarian	Peer Leader	Submissiveness to Peer Leader
1	⊕			
2	⊕			
3	⊕			
4	⊕	⊕	+ O	
5	⊕	⊕	+ O	
6	⊕	⊕	+ O	+
7	⊕	⊕	+ O	+
Types of Behaviour	Accept ideas Ask questions Direct activity Answer in response Seek help	Warn Disapprove Raise hand	Response to peers' deviance	

Key
+ represents 40 per cent or greater acknowledgement of specific authority.
0 represents behavioural actions typical of specific authority.

Figure 5.2 *Combined results of knowledge and behaviour studies.*

ledge. The child comes to 'know' the happenings of her/his environment.

The second scheme of development is characterised in the *Teacher as Disciplinarian* column. The reader will notice immediately that disciplinary behaviours and realisation of such behaviours occurred simultaneously (as well as peer–peer interactions and deviance). The co-occurrence of action/realisation may be cited as a social example of concrete operational schemes. The children were able to make a simultaneous understanding/realisation when action occurred. The recognition of the disciplinary functions of the teacher necessarily occurred with teachers' discipline-oriented behaviours. These behaviours appear to be caused by a formalising of the primary school curriculum, children's dual-centredness (to teacher and peer) and related tensions between child and teacher. Formalisation of the curriculum represents the movement to more individually defined subject areas and specific syllabuses to be completed. Children begin to show an inquisitiveness about other people's activities and social thoughts. The tension to work towards the completion of the syllabuses becomes exaggerated if the teacher has to spend time reminding pupils to continue their work rather than talk with their neighbours. ·
Insights from the combined studies point to the role that behavioural

actions (and, hence, ritualised relationships) play in the formation of the child's social understanding. Simply, the child learns by doing. All too often the 'doing' has only been interpreted as verbal doing, but one must also be aware of the effect of behavioural actions. Teachers and pupils act and interact in the tightly defined classroom situation. Behaviours by one or the other are acknowledged in the child's realisation of the teacher. The process of realisation (its repetition or immediacy) is mediated by the schemes of development to which the child has access.

PERCEPTUAL UNDERSTANDING OF SCHOOL AUTHORITY

The previous parts of the study have illuminated action-realisation schemes of development. But the study was not so comprehensive as to illuminate the extent and range of children's knowledge of parental, teacher and leader authority and how this knowledge facilitated further development. Questions explored some previously un-answered development phenomena, but raised more specific queries such as: if teaching responsibilities were not recognised by children in the reception class, how was this person perceived? Did parents contribute towards this understanding? How was the term 'leader' originally used? What insights might this provide about the constraining figure described by the children? And, underlying the development of authority, was there a structural coherence to the powers of figures chosen for interview, and how does this coincide with the previous literature cited on authority?

In this further section of the study 56 children (28 male, 28 female) from schools representing working and middle classes were inter-viewed individually. Children ranged in age from 4:8 to 11:6. The interviewing procedure used the pictures from the 'Knowledge of School Authority' study. Mothers, fathers and teachers were identified for all the children. Results were obtained from the clinical-projective method of interview. Categories used for comparison were generated from the children's answers, and the interviews (on tape) were retro-spectively coded. The answers that the children provided were grouped into: (1) how they identified the authority figures; (2) the role and responsibility of authority figures; (3) the range or aspects of authority asserted by the figures (the types and definitions were adopted from Wood, 1968). Findings are reported by sex, social class and developmental differences of the individual groupings and then integrated into a fuller perspective of development.

(1) *Identification of Authority Figure*
Conclusions that may be drawn from this section are very limited. Each of the children interviewed was shown each of the pictures (see

Appendix 1). During probing as to how the child identified parent, teacher, or leader, the following categories of response were generated:

Location: position of figure in picture.
Clothing: type of dress worn by figure.
Size/Age: physical or aged appearance of figure.
Neutral Activity: ⁣ some action taking place, such as walking, talking.
Authoritative Action: acknowledgement that figure has some form of control over other figures in picture.
Other Presence: acknowledgement and labelling of other people in picture.

Results were compared by category; no significant differences due to sex or social class of the children were found. Table 5.6 sets out developmental differences in the identification of authority figures. Significant differences were found in the acknowledgement of other presence (of children), in parent and leader, and in the authoritative action of leader. The results showed that identification of the figures developed from physical descriptions to acknowledgement of personal and psychological attributes. The reader will note that the identification of the figure has moved from a simple location/size (figurative) to an interpersonal action basis (operative), a finding generally supported in social-cognition literature. The teacher was identified by both location in the classroom and by the presence of pupils. The acknowledgement of others is interesting in that the children usually cited others in (reciprocal) response to the presence of the authority figure (e.g. 'The father is telling them off', 'They are writing sums that teacher has told them'). A figure of authority must have someone over whom to assert that authority. The person under control must be aware of the authority of the former figure.

(2) *Range and Aspects of Authority*
The types and definitions of authority noted by Wood (1968) provided a basis to compare range and development of the power/authority of the figures. The types and definitions are:

Teach: conveyance of knowledge.
Control: general behavioural control/manipulation of another.
Coercive Control: behavioural manipulation under threat of punishment.
Moral Control: control with right or wrong stressed as a factor.
Care: child is looked after.
Kind: figure gives something (e.g. a present) to, or does something for, child.

Table 5.6 *Identification of Parent, Teacher, Leader (percentages by age-grouping)*

Locate (year)	Parent	Teacher	Leader	Neutral Act (year)	Parent	Teacher	Leader
1	0·0	37·5	0·0	1	0·0	25·0	0·0
2	0·0	87·5	12·5	2	12·5	0·0	0·0
3	0·0	75·0	37·5	3	12·5	0·0	0·0
4	12·5	37·5	25·0	4	12·5	0·0	0·0
5	12·5	75·0	50·0	5	12·5	0·0	12·5
6	0·0	37·5	37·5	6	25·0	25·0	0·0
7	12·5	62·5	25·0	7	37·5	37·5	25·0

Clothing (year)				Authoritative (year)			
1	37·5	12·5	0·0	1	12·5	0·0	0·0
2	50·0	12·5	0·0	2	0·0	0·0	12·5
3	25·0	0·0	0·0	3	12·5	25·0	25·0
4	75·0	12·5	0·0	4	12·5	25·0	25·0
5	37·5	0·0	0·0	5	25·0	25·0	37·5
6	25·0	0·0	0·0	6	25·0	37·5	75·0
7	12·5	0·0	0·0	7	37·5	25·0	50·0

Size/Age (year)				Other Presence (year)			
1	12·5	0·0	12·5	1	0·0	12.5	0·0
2	0·0	0·0	0·0	2	0·0	37·5	0·0
3	25·0	0·0	12·5	3	0·0	50·0	12·5
4	0·0	0·0	50·0	4	25·0	62·5	25·0
5	37·5	0·0	0·0	5	50·0	62·5	37·5
6	12·5	25·0	12·5	6	50·0	62·5	75·0
7	12·5	0·0	12·5	7	75·0	62·5	75·0

Help: child and figure work together to solve problem, etc.
Dislike: child is critical of authority figure.

Results were compared by category; no significant differences were found due to sex or social class of the children. Table 5.7 sets out the developmental differences in the figures and authority acknowledged. Significant developmental differences were found in: teach (parent, leader, with teacher showing high consistency after the first year in school); control (leader, with high consistency in parent and teacher); moral (teacher, with high consistency in parent); and dislike (teacher, parent and leader). Information drawn from Table 5.7 provides several insights into development. The primary role of teacher was

The Three-Part Study and its Results / 81

Table 5.7   *Range and Aspects of Authority of Figures (Parent, Teacher, Leader) (percentage by age-grouping)*

Teach (year)	Parent	Teacher	Leader	Help (year)	Parent	Teacher	Leader
1	0·0	12·5	0·0	1	0·0	0·0	0·0
2	12·5	100·0	0·0	2	50·0	37·5	0·0
3	50·0	100·0	12·5	3	37·5	25·0	12·5
4	62·5	100·0	37·5	4	0·0	62·5	12·5
5	37·5	100·0	12·5	5	37·5	50·0	50·0
6	50·0	100·0	12·5	6	50·0	50·0	25·0
7	50·0	100·0	12·5	7	37·5	25·5	12·5

Control (year)	Parent	Teacher	Leader	Kind (year)	Parent	Teacher	Leader
1	100·0	75·0	0·0	1	12·5	25·0	0·0
2	87·5	87·5	62·5	2	37·5	12·5	0·0
3	100·0	100·0	75·0	3	37·5	25·0	12·5
4	100·0	100·0	87·5	4	25·0	37·5	0·0
5	100·0	100·0	100·0	5	50·0	25·0	12·5
6	100·0	100·0	100·0	6	75·0	12·5	25·0
7	100·0	100·0	75·0	7	50·0	12·5	12·5

Coercive (year)	Parent	Teacher	Leader	Dislike (year)	Parent	Teacher	Leader
1	12·5	12·5	0·0	1	0·0	0·0	0·0
2	50·0	37·5	0·0	2	0·0	0·0	0·0
3	0·0	12·5	12·5	3	0·0	0·0	0·0
4	12·5	25·0	0·0	4	0·0	0·0	0·0
5	12·5	25·0	0·0	5	0·0	37·5	0·0
6	0·0	0·0	0·0	6	62·5	37·5	37·5
7	0·0	0·0	0·0	7	0·0	12·5	25·0

Moral (year)	Parent	Teacher	Leader	Care (year)	Parent	Teacher	Leader
1	62·5	0·0	0·0	1	25·0	0·0	0·0
2	37·5	12·5	0·0	2	75·0	25·0	0·0
3	50·0	12·5	0·0	3	50·0	12·5	0·0
4	62·5	37·5	12·5	4	75·0	12·5	25·0
5	75·0	62·5	25·0	5	100·0	0·0	0·0
6	75·0	62·5	0·0	6	50·0	37·5	0·0
7	62·5	62·5	12·5	7	75·0	12·5	25·0

acknowledged after the first year in school and then generalised to both parent and leader.

Young children viewed the role of each figure as unique, with little overlap between figures. Older children were able to make comparisons between the figures. An example of the extreme separation of the schoolteacher role *v.* parental responsibility was highlighted in an interview with Simon (4:11) whose mother was a teacher. After clarifying that Simon's conception of mother was one who 'cooks' and generally looks after the house, and that teachers 'write on boards' and say 'it's playtime' among other actions, he was asked 'Are mothers and fathers and teachers the same in any way?'

Simon:	Um . . . no.
Interviewer:	Why are they different?
Simon:	Cause teachers don't stay at home and people who don't go to work stay at home.

Simon gave an answer that showed his inability to separate between the placement and responsibility of parents and teachers.

At the opposite end of the developmental scale Alexander (11:5) gave a very specific answer showing quite exacting definitions and limitations of authority.

Interviewer:	Do you think that mothers and fathers and teachers are the same in any ways?
Alexander:	A few. Well yeah . . . really in some ways. Um, teacher is in charge of a class and mothers and fathers are in charge of their children.
Interviewer:	OK, and how would they be different?
Alexander:	Um, well a teacher has to teach the children more, you know . . . lots of things about the school and learning and all that, and mothers and fathers are, you know, teach you a little bit, but are really . . . er . . . to look after you.

The older child showed clear delineation of parental and teacher responsibility. Additionally, he was able to note similarity between their roles. In all the interviews the ability to teach was primarily (and initially) the concern of the teacher and later generalised to parent and leader.

The range of authority of parents included general behavioural control, moral criteria for good or bad, helping and caring. Children in the 4½–6½ years age-range described teachers using the same criteria as those they used to describe parents. Either the teacher was seen as the same as parent, or there appeared to be a general perception of the adult who was in a position of power with which the child must function. The similarity in young children's perception of parents and teachers undoubtedly helped in the child's entry to school. At entry to primary school a secure and affectionate relationship with adults was the basis for accepting and relating to the teacher. This assertion was supported through all the interviews with the youngest children when the question was asked 'Do you like parents (teachers)?' The universal answer was 'Yes'. When probed, the youngest children answered 'I like——because I do'. Or they referred to some action basis such as 'They help me do things (get dressed, tie shoes, etc.)'. Older children gave more specific answers, noting separate criteria for responsibilities of caring, upbringing and education. On the whole, the children maintained a liking for the authority figures. The initial similarity in perception of parent and teacher showed how an adult with power (with specific contact with the child) was heeded, trusted and uncritically 'liked' by the child. This perception of authority helped to ease the child into the reception class – a further example of Stayton *et al.*'s (1971) 'predisposition for obedience'.

Upon entering the school, the child quickly learned of the instructional responsibility of the teacher. After this responsibility was acknowledged it was quickly reflected on to parents. The ability to reflect back (or in a way, generalise) was limited to adults close to the child. The development of the leader concept lagged far behind parent and teacher. When the child started describing the leader, that person was seen as having similar responsibilities to those of parent and teacher. The leader did not display any new or vitally different aspect of authority. The leader's authority was the same constraining power relationship over children which was noted in the 'Knowledge of School Authority' part of the study.

The assertion of power and control over children was characteristic of each of these figures of authority. One may be surprised by the general lack of criticism or dislike of this state of affairs. But these findings only support previous speculations that power realisation is based upon a trusting/affective relationship. It is hard for children to dislike someone whom they love. It appears, then, that authority perception and understanding are based upon initial social-emotional factors and generalised through the experiences of childhood. Some form of trust is initially perceived in an individual, allowing further contact. The experience of further contact, along with developing mental skills, extends and qualifies the responsibilities of this person. The realisation may then be reflected back upon other members of the child's social repertoire.

(3) *Role and Responsibility of Authority Figure*
The children's actual description of the jobs and duties of the authority figures provided greater clarity as to the development of their understanding of these figures.

(*a*) Responsibilities of parents were described by the children as:

controlling behaviour, teaching, caring, helping (as in the aspects of authority) and housework, work (away-from-the-house responsibilities), fixing/mending. Results were compared by category; no significant differences were found due to sex or social class of the children. Only the responsibility of the parent as a teacher showed a significant increase with age. In breaking down the parental responsibilities into maternal and paternal areas, strong sex stereotypes were found. Even the youngest children classically noted that the mother 'did the cooking', 'cleaned', did the 'shopping' and was generally responsible for caring for children. Fathers 'mended' things around the house and went out to 'work'. The stereotypes were surprisingly strong, especially as many mothers in the area did have jobs outside the home. Sex stereotypes appeared as a realisation by children of their own parents' activities in the home (a further example of action-realisation). (Changes in sex stereotypes in schoolbooks will, probably, have little effect unless basic home activities of parents are changed.)

(*b*) Responsibilities of teachers were generally described in the aspects of authority. Additionally, children spoke of the teacher being in the classroom, special subjects taught by particular teachers and whether they had learnt of teachers' responsibilities through their own experiences or were told about teachers by a family member. Results were compared by category; there were no significant differences due to social class. Boys stated that they learnt more about teachers from the home than did girls. Developmentally, there were differences in the recognition of special subject responsibility and general classroom control responsibilities by older children. Children gained their knowledge of teachers mainly through classroom experience and this knowledge was sensitive to the teaching specialisations as they took place in the school. The responsibility of teacher generally supported the 'Knowledge of School Authority' formulations.

(*c*) Responsibilities of leaders provided the most insight in this area of the study. Children's knowledge of leaders developed from no understanding to a very sophisticated and specific assertion of authority. Using a developmental progression, extracts from the interviews will be reported.

The youngest children had little understanding of leaders. Ian (4:10) had no understanding of the word leader.

Interviewer:	Do you know what a leader is?
Ian:	No.
Interviewer:	Do you know what leaders do?
Ian:	No.
Interviewer:	Is there a leader in the pictures?
Ian:	No.

A more sophisticated answer was provided by Simon (4:11).

Interviewer:	Can you tell me what a leader is?
Simon:	(No response)
Interviewer:	Do you know what leaders do?
Simon:	They lead you.
Interviewer:	What sort of things do they lead you in?
Simon:	They lead you into the Hall.
Interviewer:	How does a person become a leader?
Simon:	Someone tells them to.
Interviewer:	Who tells them to be a leader?
Simon:	(No response)

For Simon a leader is the person at the head of a line that moves from one room to another in school. That leader is an appointed individual (usually by the authority present, i.e. the teacher).

Ruth (5:10) expanded about the leader as found in school.

Interviewer:	What do leaders do?
Ruth:	Well, a leader takes people places.
Interviewer:	OK, where do you find leaders?
Ruth:	Don't know . . .
Interviewer:	How does a person become a leader?
Ruth:	Well, teacher tells them and then they become a leader.
Interviewer:	Do leaders do anything special?
Ruth:	Dinner leaders do.
Interviewer:	What do they do?
Ruth:	They tell us when dinner is ready for our table to go . . .

For Ruth leaders were teacher appointments. They headed lines and had specific school dinner responsibilities.

Michael's (9:4) understanding of 'leader' moved outside the classroom.

Interviewer:	What do leaders do?
Michael:	They're a sort of boss and tell you things . . .
Interviewer:	Are there any leaders in the classroom?
Michael:	No.
Interviewer:	Where would you find a leader?

Michael:	Police station, fire station, officer.

For Michael the leader had evolved out of the classroom and taken on responsibility for society.

Alexander (11:5) expanded on a leader's group responsibilities and the development of the concept.

Interviewer:	Where do you usually find leaders?
Alexander:	Cub pack . . . or a gang.
Interviewer:	What do leaders do?
Alexander:	Well, they're in charge of people in a group. They shouldn't really boss them about, but they are in charge. They make most of the plans and things like that, or what you're going to do.
Interviewer:	How does a person become a leader?
Alexander:	Well, it depends, like if it was a group of boys and girls like that, they sometimes choose a leader, or sometimes they might vote for it, or maybe it might be the person who started the actual game.
Interviewer:	How do you know about leaders?
Alexander:	I don't know. I've been a leader a few times in my school . . . and I used to be in the games.

The actual concept of leader has been shown to develop from a teacher-appointed position for movement between rooms to a near-democratic concept requiring choosing and voting. For a clearer representation of this development, the interviews were analysed for categories generated from the children.

Responsibilities of a Leader
In the school: as found in lines, school meals, games, etc.
Boss: give orders to subordinates that are to be followed.
Plan: prepare for events.
Teach: conveyance of knowledge.
Help: child and figure work together to solve problem, etc.

Background to the Child's Learning about Leader; Leaders Acknowledged in . . .
Lines: for movement from room to room in schools.
Games: in the school, including physical education.
Head of school.
Scouts.
Gangs: children's groups or criminal groups.
Industry: boss or foreman at work.
Police.

Government: prime minister, president, elected representative.

How a Person Becomes a Leader
Succession
Voting
Original group member
Most popular member of a group
Strongest
Work towards leadership
Educated for leadership.

Results were analysed by category. Table 5.8 displays differences of statistical significance.

Leaders were initially and consistently seen in schools, primarily in lines and then in games. Leadership was then seen in school administration, police, scouts and gangs. Leadership was constantly described in terms of dominance, with children following orders. A few older children mentioned that some leaders may be elected. But a vast majority maintained the early usage of 'leader': that of teacher (or adult) appointment. Responsibilities of this leader were based on adult-oriented constraint. The child's understanding of leader was not the democratic concept that political socialisation theories might have us believe. Leadership simply replicated adult power relationships.

STRUCTURE OF AUTHORITY: A GENERAL PERSPECTIVE

The child's introduction to and interaction with members of the primary school expand awareness of the social/authority world of adults and peers. The series of studies presented here describes the social experience of the child in the classroom. The studies sought schemes by which the child adapted to entry to the primary school. Upon entry the child demonstrated an affective tie towards the teacher. The teacher was described as being similar to parents. The

Table 5.8   *Significant Differences in Leader Categories*

Category	Type of Difference	Level of Significance
Boss	Developmental	0·001
Plan	Developmental	0·033
Help	Developmental	0·05
Police	Sex (male > female)	0·02
Strong	Sex (male > female)	0·017
Work	Class (MC > WC)	0·005
Head	Developmental	0·028
Gang	Developmental	0·001

affective or trusting relationship transferred from parent to teacher was further demonstrative of a 'disposition for obedience'. The generation of this relationship of love and obedience may lie in early upbringing practices. The outcome of the relationship was the child's understanding and acceptance of a dominant power position of constraint. The child's position in this relationship was one of (initial) unquestioning acceptance of parent or teacher.

When exploring the developing understanding of teacher, one must be aware of the limited set of behaviours available to child and teacher (which precede a *de facto* understanding of the authority of teachers). The limited set of behaviours may be described as ritualised or habitualised (which were pre-operatively realised by the child). Thus, the developing social world of the child was a paradox. The child was an active constructor and construer of the social world but behavioural actions were strictly limited. *De facto* realisation was not limited to pre-operative schemes, for evidence has also been produced for more immediate and concrete realisation of behaviours (e.g. disciplinary functions of the teacher). The child's relationship with teacher was realised (developmentally) through interactions with members of the child's environment and rituals for those interactions. From the acceptance of an affective relationship with the teacher to the realisation of the role and responsibilities of the teacher, the child played an active role. The processes which helped promote the realisation were that of action and affect forming an example of *social decalage*.

The child's understanding of leadership provided further examples of pre-operative and concrete schemes. Initial knowledge of leaders was gained in early classroom experiences, such as lines and games. As the concept of leader developed from a simple teacher (or adult) appointee, the power/authority relationship remained similar to the constraining relation of the child with adult. Leadership interviews did provide evidence of advancement in children's thought. The children realised that it was their responsibility to follow the dictates and directions of the leader. Leadership derived from adult-oriented (and usually adult-appointed) experiences. The limited role of peers and the peer group in the classroom was often in conflict with the teacher-perceived running of that classroom. In the conflict that the peer group did promote, there was little evidence of the mutual or co-operative alternative described in Chapter 2. The net effect of the peer group in the classroom was to exaggerate conflict between teacher and pupil and to provide examples of equally constraining alternatives in authority for the child. Implications of the above will be drawn out in Chapter 6.

A close parallel can be drawn between the authority data presented here and the Early Authority Levels (Damon) described in Chapter 2. Table 5.9 presents a developmental progression of children's concep-

Table 5.9   *Progression of Children's Conception of Authority*

Stage 1
This level is almost taken for granted by most of the children interviewed. Characteristic conception of the authority figure is that the child likes the authority figure, but can provide no reasons for the liking. The child acknowledges that the authority figure may tell him/her to be good, but sees own actions as good. This child acknowledges parental authority, sees teacher as a nice person and has no concept of leader. Authority is perceived in the role of the individual.

Stage 2
Basic affective/liking relationship with authority figure, mainly parents. There is a tendency to describe authority figure in physical terms. Acknowledgement of control and elementary moral responsibility (bad and good). Child is still told to do things by figure. Authority personnel limited to parents and teaching responsibilities are introduced.

Stage 3
Authority figures are expanding in number. Realisation that authority figure 'does something' for the child. The child therefore ought to like the authority. As this authority is mainly limited to people close to the child (parent, teacher) there is no conflict; quite active acceptance of situation. Children are able to interact with one another. This extension of interaction brings the expression of conflict between alternative figures and realisation of a vague contractual relationship.

Stage 4
While acknowledging and accepting the constraining authority relationship, the child perceives specific use for this person or knowledge. The child may express some dislike for the authority figure, but still accepts the relationship. Dislike of the authority figure may be expressed but the contract is more fully realised (e.g. 'If we don't have teachers we won't be able to get jobs when we grow up'). Parents, teachers and leaders are acknowledged as figures of authority and all have their separate realms.

Stage 5
An expansion of Stage 4, with the realisation of childhood or adolescent authority figures. Likes and dislikes of authority figures are expressed along with contractual relations. These authorities are not challenged by the child. The potential of a child leader is qualified in that the leader is described with constraining powers similar to those of adults. The method for choosing this leader is more 'democratic' than affective, e.g. children now speak of expertise, education and possibility of voting.

tion of authority in relation to the individuals from whom they learned their authority relation. The stages of Table 5.9 are closely paralleled in Damon's levels O-A to 2-B. The table does go beyond Damon's research in that a social decalage is also presented. The decalage notes the primacy of the affective relationship between child and parent in establishing an awareness of authority. Affect promotes a trust and dependence on the parent, an obedient acceptance of the relationship, and generalises to first encounters with the teacher. Interactive experiences extend the concept of teacher to include knowledge and control functions and expand the general concept of authority. The extended knowledge is reflected back on to parents.

The experience of school introduces the child to a conflict between teacher/bureaucratic authority and the desire to get on with peers. The conflict extends the concept of teacher and provides grounds to challenge the affective basis of the relationship. Unqualified liking of the teacher is replaced by a contractual relationship, still based upon constraint (and obedience). The relationship is described in terms of the expertise of the teacher and the perceived necessity for education. The initial conception of leader has an affective basis, but it is soon developed in terms of the contractual relationship of constraint.

This chapter will be concluded by briefly noting parallels to developmental psychological research. Implications for schools and schooling are discussed in Chapter 6. The series of explorative studies undertaken here follows many of the assumptions of cognitive developmental theory. Social authority development is here shown to progress in stages. New cognitive aspects of authority are integrated into the child's repertoire. These aspects are adapted from interactive experiences with the child's social environment. While the expansion of the content of the child's repertoire is easily noted, the structure of the authority also develops. Schemes of development characteristic of pre-operative and concrete stages of cognitive development are shown to be characteristic of social-cognitive development too. Conclusions can also be drawn concerning the effect of affect in facilitating and interacting with social development. The role of affect underlying the establishment of children's relationships allows for the acceptance of and introduction to new authority figures. The relationship with parents eases introduction to the teacher, the relationship with the teacher eases introduction to the leader. The similarities in the child's initial description of these figures show how the knowledge of one leads to acceptance of the next, a description of decalage. The studies explored the type and quality of authority acknowledged by the primary school child: an authority based on an underlying powerful or less powerful relationship. While constraint appears to be the only underlying authority relationship, it may not be the only one – another topic to be taken up in Chapter 6.

Chapter 6

Summary and Conclusion

The earlier chapters in this book attempted to draw together literature on the development of the child and the context within which the development takes place. Development, itself, has multiple meanings covering aspects of physical, social and intellectual 'growth' and interactions between each of these. But the reader, as well as any parent or teacher, must be aware that this development takes place within specific contexts: generally of the home and school, and more specifically in human social relations. I have explained the growth of the child in a similar manner to Youniss's (1978) analysis, that is, by studying cognitive elements in the child's knowledge and how these relate to the context in which the knowledge has been acquired. The opening of the book, then, focused on early development and social relationships (attachment, obedience) to exemplify the cognitive/ context format. Early development further explored the development of reciprocal social relationships started in the home and continuing beyond it. Children formed partnerships with parents and peers within which they learned about their world. From parental games to peer play, qualitative changes in authority relations were realised and provided a background for the moral and social development of the child. The primary school was ultimately focused upon; for it provided the arena within which the transition from a home to a societal orientation (encompassing the social and authority relations described above) took place.

Early development sets a basic background for the child's future. The young infant (neonate) shows an early social preference for humans rather than other forms of interesting object (which may be put in terms of a biological pre-adaptation). The sensori-motor period, which covers a broad area of development from neonatal sensory experience to (cognitive) object and person permanence, has been shown to include also an affective element. The intertwining of sensory, motor, cognitive and affective elements most often takes place within a home and caretaker presence. Thus early development is placed in a sensory and sensitive context. Development may be described by cognitive (with sensory cues – signalling and recall), social (interacting with parents and caretaker) and affective (security/ dependence) formulations.

Attachment and bonding represent one aspect of the intertwined early development. The quality or intensity of the attachment relationship may vary with different upbringing environments, caretaker attitudes, child temperament, and so on. But the variance does not negate its presence and essence. Attachment does represent a two-sided relation – of caretaker to child and child to caretaker.

Early games initially repeat motor actions again and again to the point where they become regularised or habitualised. Upon realisation of a 'correct' format to the game, the child and others can vary the format and introduce new rules. Play thus allows for mastery of both physical/motor and social skills. But play most often takes place in a strict social context; while the above masteries are developed, sex stereotypes and authority relations often set the scene for play.

The child's social play is soon extended to play with peers. The introduction of peers, hypothetically, radically alters the child's understanding of power relationships (from hierarchy to co-operation). Rules can be changed or modified to suit current needs. Co-operation promotes greater social understanding (in language, perception, etc.) and contributes to the growing awareness of self and others. The availability of peers and peer play depends on whether they are nearby, are thought appropriate to play with, and similar factors.

Research concerning the developing child invariably involves some form of social interaction. Whether one looks upon the development as integrated (i.e. an amalgamation of intellectual, social, moral and authority understanding as a singular unit) or as separate and parallel developments, common elements underlie the orientations. This book has been written with an integrated orientation format, but emphasises the common elements. Common elements include: that development of social understanding moves from practical awareness of events surrounding the child to theoretical understanding of principles and laws; that the child's understanding moves from global/ego-centric to differentiation/socialised (intellectual and social realms); that early practical understanding is derived from a realisation of ritualised or habitualised actions; that development of authority relations and, hence, moral judgements is intertwined with early affective relations (e.g. there appears a reciprocal emotional bond between actors of the relationship); and that schemes of action expand and support a logical underpinning to social development.

The child's developing social relations can be characterised in terms of 'archetypical' authority relations of parents and peers. Through interactions with these individuals, the child forms a social (and moral, etc.) understanding of self, others and relationships. The stance taken throughout this book is that the amalgamation of social understanding is based upon the authority relations of constraint and co-operation. The autonomous child is able to juxtapose the two and thus form judgements. But, as confusions do inevitably arise, we must also be fully aware of the context where the juxtaposition is *allowed* to take place. Unless the child has the range of experiences cited, then the basis for forming judgements is very limited.

The primary school is just such a context. It involves the combined intensive social relationships of parents and peers in a relatively closed context (with societal rules and order). The primary school is an arena that provides an intermediary step in the child's transition from a home to societal orientation. The dual aims of the primary school are explicitly to promote intellectual as well as social development of the child. Upon first being introduced to the school the (reception aged) child will form a close relationship with the teacher. The relationship is strikingly similar to relationships with parents, showing aspects of trust and dependence. The child also realises the teacher's classroom roles and responsibilities. Introduction to a group of peers within the school also facilitates both social and intellectual development. Social effects are found in games, role-playing and general conversations among children. It is more difficult to provide precise instances of intellectual effects. We can cite the potential for the cognitive conflict generated in a group (within the numerous instances of group discussion and project work characteristic of today's primary schools). A more general survey of the primary school will also show a systematic set of authority relations between differing age-groups of children, children with adults and children with knowledge. Upon entry to school, children are introduced to a bureaucracy, certain ritualised ways of acting and a vast amount of new and organised information. All these introductions take place under the auspices of authority relations with teachers (and other adults) and peers. The schemes available to the child to understand this developing (and confusing) context add further insight into the dynamics of how the child comes to grips with this situation. The separate studies described in the previous chapter form a preliminary insight into the workings of these dynamics. The primary school is thus an arena for social and intellectual interaction which can be generally labelled as socialisation.

The series of studies reported in Chapter 5 set out to explore the development and understanding of the main social authority relations of the primary school. The study adopted a format which centred on the child's actions, interactions and verbal awareness and understanding. Children were interviewed and observed. I was able to draw upon and integrate elements of symbolic-interactionist and cognitive-developmental theories in the studies. Both the theories stress the effects of the environment (both social and physical) on the development of thought and understanding. Additionally, constraints on actions and understanding in the symbolic-interactionist theory, and the way in which action effects understanding in cognitive-developmental theory were noted. The studies explored the formal and informal relations of the child's primary school classroom environment. But by looking deeper than the surface interactions and general knowledge of the classroom, an organised picture of social power and authority was illuminated along with schemes of development. In the child's transition from home to the broader context of society these studies demonstrated parts of the process and dynamics of socialisation. Additionally, the studies brought several constraints of the primary school into close focus: teacher–pupil relationships, models of authority and competence in learning, and the broad area of social/political competence.

The study areas will be briefly summarised with the above constraints more clearly identified. They were designed to 'naturalistically' seek developmental understanding of authority relations in the primary school classroom. Elements of behavioural action, interaction and cognitive understanding of the authority relations of teacher and peer were explored. Patterns of social understanding were illuminated. These patterns demonstrated how behaviour brought about cognitive recognition and understanding of authority within the specific confines of the classroom. The study provided an explicit example of the bridge between action and knowledge (explored in the early writings of Piaget and more recently by Wohlwill and by Damon). Separate studies explored the development of knowledge, behavioural and general perceptual understanding of school authority, and how the child adapts to school relationships.

'Knowledge of Social Authority' sought developmental evidence of the child's growing understanding of teachers and peers. The interviews specifically sought to define (from the child's viewpoint) the type of authority/power relationships that were used in the classroom. Quite specific concepts of *Teacher as Teacher* and *Teacher as Disciplinarian* as well as *Leadership* and *Submissiveness* among peers were used by the children. All of these specific concepts had a common underlying feature – a hierarchical or constraining authority relationship between the pictured figures and the child. The children saw themselves as dominated by the figures. An element of reciprocity appeared in the relationships with the figures; the child acknowledged an obligation to heed the directions of the authority. Knowledge of these authority concepts appeared in a step-wise process (shown in the scalogram analysis). The process was replicated in a similar cross-cultural study. The comparison with children in Detroit showed social authority development following the same ordering in the similar environment of the primary school. But development was dependent on experience. The children in Detroit started school six months later than the London children and school authority figures were identified correspondingly six months later.

'Behavioural Actions and Interactions in the Classroom' demonstrated standard developmental differences in roles and actions of classroom members. Teachers in the early years of schooling were strongly child-centred and allowed much spontaneous action and interaction. Children sought attention and affection from these teachers and directed most of their developing communicative skills towards them. Teachers in the middle and later years of the primary school maintained several behaviours similar to teachers of younger pupils. But they also became more formal and subject-oriented. Pupils developed more specific interactions with their teachers: for example, asking questions and raising hands to respond to questions. Coincidentally, the children started speaking and interacting more spontaneously with one another. The increase in child–child interactions brought, in turn, a drastic increase in warnings and directions by the teacher. Pupils also found new ways of avoiding teacher directions. A comparison of behaviours in the primary schools in England with similar schools in Detroit showed few significant differences. The differences found showed that children from a working-class background in England were more active and received more attention than their middle-class counterparts, while the opposite results were found in the Detroit samples.

Each of the two previous studies provided insights into growth and development within the specific social context of the classroom. Combining the two studies provided an integrated view of development with much greater theoretical importance. Focusing on Figure 5.2, two distinct schemes of interactional learning were displayed. A scheme of interactive learning in which behaviours were repeated over and again until cognitively realised and understood was demonstrated in the transition from the first to the second year in school in the acknowledgement of *Teacher as Teacher*. Behaviours were the same in the first and second year classrooms while realisation lagged behind (Law of Conscious Realisation): a pre-operative scheme of social understanding was shown. The co-occurrence of warnings by the teacher and acknowledgement of the *Teacher as Disciplinarian* demonstrated the immediacy of realisation in concrete operational social schemes. Two distinctive elements of theory were shown in the combination of the above studies: (1) the child learned by behaviourally 'doing', and this 'doing' was bound by the context within which it took place; (2) the realisation/understanding of this social knowledge developed in schemes similar to (if not the same as) schemes of logical-mathematical development (Piaget and Inhelder, 1969).

The final study, 'Perceptual Understanding of School Authority', provided further verbal and action information about the development of knowledge concerning teachers and leaders. The interviews were limited by the picture/clinical technique adopted for the study. But several normative and developmental insights could be drawn from them. Identification of the authority figures by the youngest age-groups initially focused on their physical attributes. With older children identification evolved to personal and psychological attributes. Older children identified the authority figures in relation to the other figures in the pictures and gave reciprocal reasons for a display of authority (for example, 'He did something wrong', 'She is giving them directions'). The finding of movement from physical to psychological attributes is in keeping with several developmental person perception studies (for example, Livesley and Bromley, 1967).

The roles perceived and aspects of authority acknowledged by the children showed both an awareness of the distinct responsibilities and how the authorities' actions overlapped with one another. The youngest children interviewed perceived aspects of parent and teacher (adult figures) authority as centring on caring and behavioural or moral control. With the older age-groupings, the early authority aspects remained in their understanding but the specific figures became more differentiated and focused. Clearly, the *learning* of teaching responsibilities took place through classroom experience. The concept of teaching was quickly generalised to parental authority. The teacher was initially perceived as similar to parent. Teacher was later understood as having specific school-oriented responsibilities. The role and understanding of leader was a concept specifically generated within the school. Leader developed later than the adult figures, and was initially identified as a classroom appointee (to supervise and impose responsibilities dictated by the teacher). Development of the leader concept, again, appeared strongly tied to the child's behavioural experiences (mainly in the school) and strongly paralleled the authorities of parent and teacher.

In summary, the aspects of authority and role/responsibility of the authority figures found during the interviews were: (1) all authority was perceived as some form of dominance over the child; (2) the children developed their initial concepts through the behavioural interactions that they maintained with these figures; (3) initial concepts of one figure quickly generalised to other figures of authority; (4) concepts of the individual authority figures were strongly stereotypical of that individual's role in society; (5) parental authority appeared as the basic structure of the authority acknowledged. Similarity to parent helped the child's introduction to school (as shown in the closeness of the initial perception of teacher to the established perception of parents).

A review of the combined studies on social and school authority indicated a strong stage developmental understanding of authority. The five stages (listed in Chapter 5) described the progression and increasingly critical understanding of the authority of constraint. The early perception of authority (Stage 1) was based on the controlling nurturant actions of parents. Reciprocally, the child's acceptance of this authority was based upon a positive affective state (love) for parents. The affective tie to parent eased the child's introduction to school (and social) authority (Stage 2): an example of horizontal decalage in a social context. The affective tie to authority may be seen as the reason for, and demonstration of, Stayton *et al.*'s (1971) 'disposition of obedience' in children. Introduction to the school and the expansion of the child's knowledge of authority figures took place through a scheme of interaction-realisation similar to pre-operational thought. Stage 3 understanding of authority moved away from the affective tie to a logical, contractual arrangement. The child realised that the authority figure provided a service for her/him and, reciprocally, the service ought to be appreciated. The child asserted a more active role in the constraining relationship of Stage 4, perceiving strict limitations on the type of authority assertion by the figure. The limitations were initially perceived in an emotional context. Incidents of a teacher stopping a child from doing some action caused the child to express dislike towards the teacher. The limitations of authority in Stage 4 were immediately linked (temporarily) with the behavioural actions which prompted the children's expressed dislike: a social example of concrete operational schemes. Stage 5 qualified the limitations of authority and its acceptance by defining a contractual obligation to accept authority. The Stage 5 contracts appeared necessary for the child's understanding and acceptance of leaders: a constraining but peer-oriented authority.

The combined studies of the development of social authority have shown: (1) stages of understanding proceed from home-oriented, affect-based, reciprocal relationships in the establishment of authority to a contract-based acceptance and understanding; (2) schemes of development are based upon social interaction which parallels logical mathematical development; (3) social decalage allows for the introduction and acceptance of new authority figures through their reflection of the qualities of known figures of authority; (4) understanding of authority is based on the *de facto* power relationship between the child and the figure of authority characterised in the social context and relationships; (5) the authority relationships of home, school and leadership are dominated by constraint.

SOME THEORETICAL IMPLICATIONS

Most of the cognitive developmental grounding and conclusions of this study has been discussed in relation to the specific study areas. Further general implications were supported throughout the study. Among the implications was the qualification that development in early and middle childhood takes place within a social context. Methodologies ought to be sensitive to the actions (including primarily behaviours) and knowledge (behavioural and cognitive-verbal) of children in specific situations and to how the action and knowledge interact. Studies which are sensitive to action or knowledge, such as those previously described, do support Vygotsky's (1967) contention that development takes place in a social context (and, as in play, the child is perpetually acting in rule-based confines – while not being immediately aware of the rules or cognitive limitations of his role, behaviour, etc.). Through acting and interacting in a social context the child comes to a gradual understanding of rules, roles and social knowledge: an example of Piaget's 'Law of Conscious Realisation'. The child's interactions with other individuals bring about the realisation and understanding of a power relationship and its characterisation in authority (and its presence in all relationships). The study has described different modes of 'Conscious Realisation' which I have qualified in terms of social equivalents of pre-operational and concrete operational schemes. Drawing together these implications, the reader can see the child actively constructing and interacting with the social world. The social world imposed specific constraints on the child in allowing specific contexts and relationships to occur. The child's means of adapting to the social world (within the limited context to which he has access) introduces specific moral and authority relations which shape future social understanding.

The findings from the study also provide a background against which a theory of close social relations may be outlined. The phrase 'close social relations' is used to differentiate affect-based relationships that the child maintains with a few individuals from general relations with others. General social relations may be seen as relationships without the basis of trust or dependence. Individuals who are included in close social relationships are those with whom the child forms some bond or attachment (within Western cultures these are usually parents initially, but extend to relatives, siblings, teachers). The close relationship has a basis in authority, which is founded on a power relationship. The reader should bear in mind that, as Piaget has noted, the power relationship may be of two basic types – constraint and co-operation – dependent on culturally determined methods of upbringing and interactions.

Within the child's developmental understanding of social and school authority, the study has identified pre-operational and concrete operational schemes by which the child expands and qualifies the authority of the school and home. From these insights two further implications for development can be drawn: (1) conceptions of authority will move towards an abstract or formal operational stage with age and experience, as shown in political socialisation literature; (2) the early development of the authority relationship must lie in the early sensori-motor schemes of infancy. The reader should be reminded that sensori-motor is an affective as well as logical stage of development (as described by Stern, 1977, and by Piaget, 1951). The affective nature of this stage has been researched elsewhere in the literature on attachment and bonding, in studies which discuss and describe reciprocal trust, security and dependence between infant and caretaker. While providing for the establishment of a primary bond, the affective tie also lies at the root of the child's initial acceptance of authority. The realisation of the power relationship takes place in a positive atmosphere of security, dependence and trust of the infant towards the caretaker which initiates uncritical (reciprocal) acceptance of it. The sensori-motor-affective basis of the authority relationship (and, for that matter, close social relationships) forces an expansion of the five stages of conception of authority described in Chapter 5. The expansion is the addition of a Stage 0 which would introduce the existence of a power relationship and the infant's affective tie (or bonding) to the figure or figures who provide caretaking. The existence of Stage 0 adds insight and a basis for establishment and child's participation in obedience, authority, moral, social and political development. Stage 0 is the unique quality which separates close social from social relationships. The developing stages, characteristic schemes of adaptation and power orientation of each stage are laid out in Table 6.1 below for ease of comparison.

IMPLICATIONS FOR SCHOOL AND SOCIAL DEVELOPMENT

The role of the primary school is to promote the intellectual and social development of the child. Such development is not a mere product of the curriculum. The primary school involves children and adults interacting with one another in a particular context. The primary school is the main vehicle for drawing the child out of the home and introducing him/her into a fully functioning social world – a world where parents no longer judge right and wrong – a world where the child is supposed to develop into an autonomously functioning being. Initial entry to the school is eased by the affective quality of the child's relationship with the first teacher. The child's developing knowledge and understanding of the teacher quickly extend and qualify the realm of social authority beyond the home. Interaction with the teacher introduces intellectual knowledge, expertise and specific behavioural controls. The primary school also introduces and establishes an interacting relationship between the child and peers. Effects of the peer group on the primary school aged child include promotion of social communication skills and intellectual and moral development. The primary school, as stressed throughout this book, initiates the child into a wide set of interactions and social relationships. In catering for

Table 6.1   *Conception of Authority*

Stages of Conception of Authority	Logical-Mathematical and Social Schemes of Adaptation	Power Orientation
0 Sensori-motor-affect with caretakers	Sensori-motor	Constraint
1 Controlling, nurturance (usually quality of parents)	Pre-operative	Constraint
2 Affective liking of authority figure (parent or teacher)	Pre-operative	Constraint
3 Logical, contractual relationship with authority figure	Concrete operational	Constraint
4 Critical acceptance of authority figure, limitation of responsibility	Concrete operational	Constraint
5 Perception of contractual relationship extending beyond immediate people with whom child has contact	Formal	Constraint

the child's social and intellectual development, the school places the child in a specific role in which patterns of authority, elements of bureaucracy and initial political society are adapted. But, given an understanding of the means by which the child develops (from the study), the relationships of the primary school severely limit the child's advance towards autonomy and competence.

The school is a very active social-learning environment for the child. This study has described and shown how the child initially adapts to the school. The child enters primary school pre-adapted to accept authority (of the teacher) through the initial affective understanding of adults. The teacher, simultaneously, maintains a nurturant role while also introducing intellectual and social skill development. The child's realisation of the specific responsibilities of the teacher develops through interaction and is acknowledged in social schemes. The social schemes, which parallel logical-mathematical schemes, are demonstrated in the acknowledgement of teacher roles of intellectual, or expert, and behavioural controller. The adaptation process (with developing schemes) is qualified by the context in which the process takes place: in this case the ritualised behaviours of the primary school classroom. The initial realisation and acknowledgement of the peer authority of the leader is similarly confined to the context and authority relations of the school. The constraining authority of the leader is the antithesis of the role as seen by teachers and educators. Leaders are certainly used by teachers for the movement (in lines) of children from one area to another. Of more importance is the fact that leaders are used in school games and sports – the activities which teachers use to 'promote co-operation and co-operative skills' among children. By assessing the children's perceived knowledge of their own activities, a quite different perception is found when compared to the teachers' ideal.

School authorities acknowledged by the children are confined to the power relationship of constraint. While constraint is predominant, the reader should not conclude that co-operative elements do not exist. Observers will detect that children with more than one year of school experience develop communication skills in their child–child inter-actions. In my study children are seen gradually to become more aware of one another. They start to shift their socialised communication skills (question-asking, responding to requests, etc.) from a predominant teacher orientation to a dual teacher and peer orientation.

This shift in orientation enables more effective communications (and hence learning) among children. Peer-oriented communications are also at the root of many classroom disruptions, causing delay in timetables and learning progress, and corresponding disciplinary ac-tions by the teacher. Placing deviant behaviours of the classroom in this communicative interactional context, an alternative explanation for the (one or two) 'bad children' or social deviants in the classroom can be gleaned. If most children fully establish their peer-oriented (and dual-centred) communications at approximately 7–8 years of age, a sequence of interaction/teacher reaction leading to the generation of the *Teacher as Disciplinarian* authority is followed. But what happens when a child's communicative skills are developed earlier and more effectively than those of the other children of the classroom? (After all, communication skills are developed through experience, and experience allows for a wide range of individual differences.) If that child has developed effective peer-oriented communication six months earlier than his/her classmates, then he/she would probably attempt to use those skills. The teacher will notice this individual child and, as often is the case, make the child an example of someone who 'needs to learn self-control'. By being focused on like this, the child's further development of communication skills may be inhibited. Given the ability to communicate with peers and threatened punishment for use of those skills, the child may begin to develop alternative means of communication; examples include waiting for the teacher to look away, and object-oriented communication (such as throwing of paper darts, rulers, etc.). From a simple conflict between the advanced social/co-operative development of the child and the classroom regi-men, deviance may result.

In order to undertand more fully the child's social development in relation to the primary school, we must consider the whole context of the school. This includes rules, authority structure, facilities for and patterns of interaction and interactors, as well as the general curriculum. The specific subject of this book has been the role of school and social authority in the development of the child. Figures of authority have been identified within the primary school along with schemes through which the child adapts to the authority. Further analysis of the types of authority has shown that all authority characterised in the primary school represents the relationship of constraint. The development of a co-operative authority is removed outside the realm of the classroom. (This is not to say that many teachers do not use the term 'co-operation'. Rather, the child's peer relations within school are dominated by examples of constraining authority among children themselves.)

The conclusion that children's social authority relationships are dominated by constraint has serious implications for social development. First, it would tend to support a purely competitive system of education, which may or may not be appropriate for society. Competition and constraint within school pushes co-operative behaviours among children outside the school, exaggerating differences in social behaviour (which take place inside and outside the school). The learning that goes on outside the school often threatens in-school learning. It is a rare teacher and school that can integrate outside learning into the classroom. Today even social behaviour outside the school appears dominated by constraint and competition, thus limiting children's social sensitivity and social competence. Secondly, the constraining authority relationship which dominates the school may inhibit the development of co-operative relationships, thus limiting the child's moral development. For the child to function at the *autonomous* stage, according to Piaget, he/she must have an equally good working knowledge and understanding of the moralities of both co-operation and constraint. Autonomy is also at the root of competence. Without autonomy one would expect to find a very dependent child. Thirdly, given that authority knowledge of the primary school aged child is limited to constraint, a serious weakness in the political socialisation process is detected. If the child's authority concept is limited to constraint, the understanding of democracy will similarly be limited to 'being told' and 'following' the leader (be it governor, president, or prime minister). Participation within the political system should not mean to simply follow when told. Participation includes active involvement in decision-making and the following-through process. Knowledge of names and positions of political figures (which is studied in political socialisation research) does not note the limitations of the authority relationship. Unless the child comes to grips with politics as a competent member of a democracy, the political system is only offering the choice of maintaining the status quo or dropping out of the system altogether (e.g. by apathy).

But, as stated before, it would be naive of me to assert that schools and teachers do not attempt to include co-operation in their class-rooms. Apart from assumed co-operation through sports and physical education, teachers have introduced group projects and peer learning strategies into their classrooms. One teacher-educator (Lickona, 1980) instructed teachers about the benefits of co-operation and found twelve distinct strategies adopted by teachers to promote co-operation in their classrooms. Strategies ranged from two-person and group tasks, to paired testing and test-taking, to reinforcement of co-operative behaviours and the teaching of altruistic skills. All strategies appeared to have some immediate effect/affect according to the teachers. While these attempts at strategies should receive the utmost in encouragement, the conclusions of the study reported in this book lead the author to challenge the effectiveness of such strategies (especially those strategies that are related to moral/social develop-ment). Conclusions arrived at in this volume pose a stage/structural basis to the development of social authority relationships. The stage/structural basis starts with the sensori-motor-affective Stage 0 and develops with verbal and logical reasoning from a home-based to expertise-based authority. Research in this volume was confined to the social authority of constraint. But we can speculate from here (as Piaget did) that the authority of co-operation would follow the same structural sequence (that is, from a sensori-motor-affective stage through pre-operative and operative stages).

Strategies used by teachers to promote co-operation are mainly based on the verbal and logical elements of the co-operative authority. But the importance of the stage theory of social authority is that the stages form an invariant hierarchical sequence, each stage being a structural whole, and with earlier stages being integrated into succeed-ing stages. Conclusions and implications arrived at in this book would posit a necessary preliminary sensori-motor-affective Stage 0 to be the basis for the co-operative authority and co-operative skills. How can this Stage 0 be incorporated into the development of the primary school aged child, especially as the child has already passed through the sensori-motor years? And how would this Stage 0 affect/effect the social/moral development of the child? To answer to the above questions I recently carried out a small-scale study (Kutnick and Brees, 1982). Children aged 4½–5 years were given sensitivity exer-cises which involved close physical contact between two children while undergoing a mildly threatening exercise (such as walking along a low balance beam or a 'blind walk' where a child is led/guided through obstacles). The exercises were chosen to promote a non-verbal sense of trust among the children, similar in quality to attachment between child and parent. They were then tested on cognitive and moral tasks (rating perceptual decentration, co-operative behaviours, competitive behaviours, and peer-versus-adult helping responses to a child in distress).

The results were compared with children who had not undertaken the exercises and to children who 'co-operated' by working together on tasks (such as puzzle-making and picture-drawing). Results indicate that those children who were able to develop an affective (through sensitivity) basis to their relationship were better able to decentre, showed significantly more co-operative behaviours and were more likely to respond to a child in distress themselves (as opposed to resorting to an adult for help). The addition of a sensori-affective basis did promote cognitive and social advancement among these children; more work is currently being planned. If the affective Stage 0 is the basis of social authority, then: (1) we can come to a better understanding of how and why individuals accept authority; (2) classroom co-operation can be enhanced by helping children build up trusting relationships among themselves, rather than just 'doing things together'; (3) given a Stage 0 basis in both constraint and co-operation, the child would be placed in a 'dialectical' position to make truly 'autonomous' moral and social judgements.

Several observations in this book may be interpreted as critical of today's primary schools. The intention behind this series of studies is just the opposite of directing more criticism at overburdened teachers. If we can understand better how individuals develop and the effect of institutions on the structuring of their thought, then we can plan for a more appropriate and effective educational system. This book attempts to expand classroom understanding by centring on social relationships and social development. Several of the implications of the study may be brought directly into the classroom. The implied development may not require a change in curriculum or teaching matter. Development is based upon the actions and interactions of children and teachers in the 'learning' context of the classroom.

Appendix 1   Pictures Used for the Interviews

Male Teacher
with Children

Female Leader
with Children

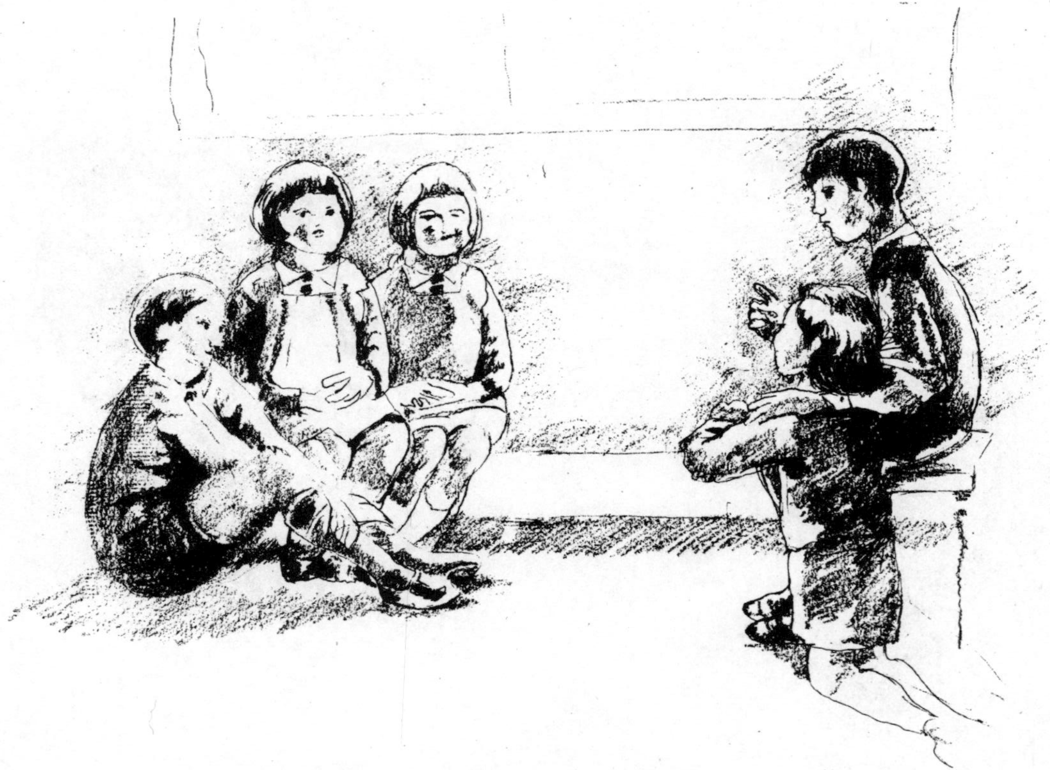

Male Leader
with Children

Children Playing

Female Adult
with Children

Male Adult
with Children

Female Teacher
with Children

Appendix 2   Observation Schedules

Table A2.1   *Flanders Teacher–Pupil Interaction Schedule (with additional deviance category)*

Teacher talk		
Indirect influence:	Accepts feelings	
	Praises or encourages	
	Accepts or uses idea of pupil	
	Asks questions	
Direct influence:	Lecturing	
	Giving directions	
	Criticising or justifying authority	
Pupil talk	Pupil talk – response to teacher	
	Pupil talk – initiated by pupil	
	Deviant act by pupil	
General activity	Silence or confusion	

Table A2.2   *Anderson and Brewer Teacher Behaviour Schedule*

Determines a detail of activity
Direct refusal
Relocating
Postponing
Disapproval
Warning
Call to attention
Rations material
Lecture method
Questions: lecture method
Perfunctory question or statement
Approval
Accepts difference
Extends invitation

Table A2.2   *Anderson and Brewer Teacher Behaviour Schedule*

Question or statement regarding child's expressed interest or activity
The build-up
Participants in joint activity
Sympathy
Permission

Table A2.3   *Anderson and Brewer Child Behaviour Schedule*

Nervous habits
Looking up
Leaving seat
Undetermined
Play with foreign object
Conforming behaviour
Child domination of child (verbal)
Child domination of child (physical)
Deviance
Respond to teacher spontaneous
Respond to teacher hand raised
Respond to teacher when called upon
Respond to teacher fail to answer
Seek help from teacher
Plan exercise with teacher
Contribute to own work (with teacher)
Contribute to others' work (with teacher)

Voluntary to peers	Response to peers
Tell experience	
Bring something	
Suggest	
Offer service	
Help	
Approve	

Appendix 3 Averaged Association and Reliability from the Observation Schedules (probability of association in brackets)

Schedule	Association		Reliability	
Teacher–pupil interaction	0·80	(0·01)	0·87	(0·05)
Teacher behaviour	0·81	(0·01)	0·96	(0·01)
Child behaviour	0·85	(0·001)	0·81	(0·05)

The test for association compared the results of each observation schedule with the two other administrations of the schedule in each classroom (the reader will remember that each schedule was administered three times in each of the classrooms observed). After the comparison of schedules in each classroom was completed, an average of the associations was made for each of the three types of schedule. Upon calculating the averaged association for each schedule, the probability of achieving a significant association was tested using Kendall's Concordance. A check for the reliability of each schedule was made by comparing different observers' rating of the same behaviours at the same time. Spearman's Rho was used to test the significance of association between the observers.

Appendix 4 Significant Differences in Observed Behaviour – Social Class

Schedule	Category of Behaviour	Level of Significance	Social Class with Greatest Frequency of Observed Behaviour
Teacher–pupil interaction	Corrective feedback	0·02	Working class
Teacher behaviour	Questioning about activity	0·01	Working class
	Determining activity	0·01	Working class
Child behaviour	Seek help	0·01	Working class

To obtain the significant differences above, the frequency of occurrence of the behaviour in each category (from each schedule) was compared between schools representative of working- and middle-class communities. A Friedman Analysis of Variance was used to test for significant differences.

Bibliography

Adelman, C., and Walker, R. (1975), *A Guide to Classroom Observation* (London: Methuen).

Aitken, M., Bennett, S. N., and Hesketh, J. (1981), 'Teaching styles and pupil progress: a re-analysis', *British Journal of Educational Psychology*, vol. 51, pp. 107–86.

Amidon, E., and Flanders, N. (1961), 'The effects of direct and indirect teacher influence on dependent-prone students of geometry', *Journal of Educational Psychology*, vol. 52, pp. 286–91.

Amidon, E., and Hough, J. (eds) (1967), *Interaction Analysis: Theory, Research and Application* (Reading, Mass.: Addison-Wesley).

Anastasi, A. (1961), *Psychological Testing* (New York: Macmillan).

Anderson, H., and Brewer, J. (1946), *Studies of Teachers' Classroom Personalities*, Vol. 2 (Stanford, Calif.: Stanford University Press).

Anderson, H., Brewer, J., and Reed, M. (1946), *Studies of Teachers' Classroom Personalities*, Vol. 3 (Stanford, Calif.: Stanford University Press).

Aronson, E., and Dunfield, J. (1973), unpublished data, Edinburgh University, cited in *Development in Infancy*, T. Bower (San Francisco: Freeman, 1974), p. 119.

Aronson, E., and Rosenbloom, S. (1971), 'Space perception in early infancy; perception within a common audiovisual space', *Science*, vol. 172, pp. 1161–3.

Baldwin, J. (1906), *Social and Ethical Interpretations of Mental Development* (New York: Macmillan).

Barnes, D. (1976), *From Communication to Curriculum* (Harmondsworth: Penguin).

Bell, R. Q. (1968), 'A reinterpretation of the direction of effects in studies of socialisation', *Psychological Review*, vol. 75, pp. 81–95.

Bennett, N. (1976), *Teaching Styles and Pupil Progress* (London: Open Books).

Bernstein, B. (1960), 'Language and social class', *British Journal of Sociology*, vol. 11, pp. 271–6.

Blurton Jones, N. (1976), 'Rough-and-tumble play among nursery school children', in *Play*, ed. J. Bruner, A. Jolly and K. Sylva (Harmondsworth: Penguin), pp. 352–63.

Bower, T. (1974), *Development in Infancy* (San Francisco: Freeman).

Bower, T. (1977), *The Perceptual World of the Child* (London: Fontana/Open Books).

Bower, T., and Wishart, J. (1973), 'Development of audio-manual coordination', cited in T. Bower, *Development in Infancy* (San Francisco: Freeman, 1974), p. 119.

Bowles, S., and Gintes, H. (1976), *Schooling in Capitalist America* (New York: Basic Books).

Brim, O., Jr (1966), 'Socialization through the life cycle', in *Socialization After Childhood*, ed. O. Brim, Jr, and S. Wheeler (New York: Basic Books), pp. 1–51.

Bronfenbrenner, U. (1974), *Two Worlds of Childhood: US and USSR* (Harmondsworth: Penguin).

Brophy, J., and Good, T. (1974), *Teacher–Student Relationships: Causes and Consequences* (New York: Holt, Rinehart & Winston).

Brown, J., Montgomery, R., and Barclay, J. (1969), 'An example of the psychological management of teacher reinforcement procedures in the elementary classroom', *Psychology in Schools*, vol. 6, pp. 336–40.

Bruner, J. (1974), 'The organisation of early skilled action', in *The Integration of a Child into a Social World*, ed. M. P. Richards (Cambridge: Cambridge University Press), pp. 167–84.

Bruner, J., and Sherwood, V. (1976), 'Peekaboo and the learning of rule structures', in *Play*, ed. J. Bruner, A. Jolly and K. Sylva (Harmondsworth: Penguin), pp. 277–85.

Bryant, P. (1974), *Perception and Understanding in Young Children* (London: Methuen).

Bull, N. (1969), *Moral Judgement from Childhood to Adolescence* (London: Routledge & Kegan Paul).

Burns, R. B. (1979), *The Self Concept* (London: Longman).

Butcher, H. J. (1965), 'The attitudes of student teachers to education; a comparison with the attitudes of experienced teachers and a study of the changes during training course', *British Journal of Social and Clinical Psychology*, vol. 4, pp. 17–24.

Cartwright, C., and Cartwright, G. (1974), *Developing Observation Skills* (New York: McGraw-Hill).

Chanan, G., and Delamont, S. (eds) (1975), *Frontiers of Classroom Research* (Windsor: NFER).

Cole, M., and Scribner, S. (1974), *Culture and Thought* (New York: Wiley).

Cooper, B. (1976), *Bernstein's Codes: A Classroom Study*, Occasional Paper No. 6 (Falmer: University of Sussex, Education Area).

Coopersmith, S. (1967), *The Antecedents of Self Esteem* (San Francisco: Freeman).

Cortis, G. (1970), 'The assessment of a group of teachers in relation to their scores on psychological tests, their college grades and certain biographical and demographic data', PhD thesis, University of London, Institute of Education.

Damon, W. (1977), *The Social World of the Child* (San Francisco: Jossey-Bass).

Davis, D., and Levine, G. (1970), 'The behavioural manifestations of teacher's expectations', unpublished manuscript, Hebrew University of Jerusalem.

Delamont, S. (1976), *Interaction in the Classroom* (London: Methuen).

Denzin, N. (1977), *Childhood Socialization* (San Francisco: Jossey-Bass).

Dewey, J. (1949), *Education and Experience* (New York: Macmillan).

Dion, K., Berscheid, E., and Walster, E. (1972), 'What is beautiful is good', *Journal of Personality and Social Psychology*, vol. 24, pp. 285–90.

Docking, J. (1980), *Control and Discipline in Schools* (London: Harper & Row).

Donaldson, M. (1978), *Children's Minds* (London: Fontana).

Douglas, J. (1964), *The Home and the School* (London: MacGibbon & Kee).

Dreeban, R. (1967), 'The contribution of schooling to the learning of norms', *Harvard Education Review*, vol. 37, pp. 211–37.

Dubin, E., and Dubin, R. (1963), 'The authority inception period in socialisation', *Child Development*, vol. 34, pp. 885–98.

Dunkin, M., and Biddle, B. (1974), *The Study of Teaching* (New York: Holt, Rinehart & Winston).

Eggleston, J. (1979), 'The construction of deviance in school', in *Schools, Pupils and Deviance*, ed. L. Barton and R. Meigham (Nafferton, Driffield: Nafferton Books), pp. 33–42.

Elkin, F., and Handel, G. (1960), *The Child and Society: The Process of Socialisation* (New York: Random House).

Erikson, E. (1972), *Childhood and Society* (Harmondsworth: Penguin).

Evans, K. (1962), *Sociometry and Education* (London: Routledge & Kegan Paul).

Fantz, R. (1961), 'The origin of form perception', *Science*, vol. 204, pp. 66–72.

Fantz, R., Ordy, J., and Udelf, M. (1962), 'Maturation of pattern vision in infants during the first six months', *Journal of Comparative and Physiological Psychology*, vol. 55, pp. 907–17.

Feshback, N. (1969), 'Student teacher preferences for elementary school pupils varying in personality characteristics', *Journal of Educational Psychology*, vol. 60, pp. 126–32.

Flanders, N. (1970), *Analysing Teacher Behavior* (Reading, Mass.: Addison-Wesley).

Flanders, N., and Haviemaki, S. (1960), 'The effect of teacher–pupil contacts involving praise on the sociometric choices of students', *Journal of Educational Psychology*, vol. 51, pp. 65–8.

Flavell, J. (1974), *Cognitive Development* (Englewood Cliffs, NJ: Prentice-Hall).

Flavell, J., Botkin, P., Fry, C., Jr, Wright, J., and Jarvis, P. (1968), *The Development of Role-Taking and Communication Skills in Children* (New York: Wiley).

Fraser, W. (1964), 'Moral education in the UK, USA and the USSR', *Aspects of Education*, vol. 1, pp. 57–67.

Freud, S. (1965), *Group Psychology and the Analysis of the Ego* (New York: Bantam Books).

Furst, N., and Amidon, E. (1967), 'Teacher–pupil interaction patterns in the elementary classroom', in *Interaction Analysis: Theory, Research and Application*, ed. E. Amidon and J. Hough (Reading, Mass.: Addison-Wesley), pp. 167–75.

Furth, H. (1978), 'Young children's understanding of society', in *Issues in Childhood Social Development*, ed. H. McGurk (London: Methuen), pp. 228–56.

Furth, H., and Wachs, H. (1974), *Thinking Goes to School* (New York: Oxford University Press).

Galton, M., Simon, B., and Croll, P. (1980), *Inside the Primary Classroom* (London: Routledge & Kegan Paul).

Garbarino, J., and Bronfenbrenner, U. (1976), 'The socialisation of moral judgment and behavior in cross cultural perspective', in *Moral Development and Behavior*, ed. T. Lickona (New York: Holt, Rinehart & Winston), pp. 70–83.

Garvey, C. (1977), *Play* (London: Fontana/Open Books).

Gesell, A., and Ilg, F. (1965), *The Child from Five to Ten* (London: Hamish Hamilton).

Glaser, B., and Strauss, A. (1967), *The Discovery of Grounded Theory: Strategies for Qualitative Research* (Chicago: Aldine).

Glidewell, J., Kantor, M., Smith, L., and Stringer, L. (1966), 'Socialisation and social structure in the classroom', in *Review of Child Development Research*, Vol. 2, ed. M. Hoffman and L. Hoffman (New York: Russell Sage Foundation), pp. 221–56.

Goffman, E. (1967), *Interaction Ritual* (Chicago: Aldine).

Good, T., and Grouws, D. (1972), 'Reaction of male and female teachers trainees to descriptions of elementary school pupils', Technical Report No. 62, Center for Research in Social Behavior, University of Missouri at Columbia, cited in *Teacher–Student Relationships: Causes and Consequences*, ed. J. Brophy and T. Good (New York: Holt, Rinehart & Winston, 1974).

Goslin, D. (1965), *The School in Contemporary Society* (Glenview, Ill.: Scott, Foresman).

Grace, G. (1979), *Teachers, Ideology and Control* (London: Routledge & Kegan Paul).

Green, B. (1956), 'A method of scalogram analysis using summary statistics', *Psychometrika*, vol. 21, pp. 79–88.

Greenfield, P. (1970), 'Playing peekaboo with a four-month-old: a study of the role of speech and nonspeech sounds in the formation of a visual schema', unpublished MS.

Haddon, F., and Lytton, H. (1969), 'Teaching approach and the development of divergent thinking abilities in primary schools', *British Journal of Educational Psychology*, vol. 38, pp. 171–80.

Hall, R., Lund, D., and Jackson, D. (1968), 'Effects of teacher on study behavior', *Journal of Applied Behavior Analysis*, vol. 1, pp. 1–12.

Hannam, C., Smyth, P., and Stephenson, N. (1976), *The First Year of Teaching* (Harmondsworth: Penguin).

Hargreaves, D. (1967), *Social Relations in a Secondary School* (London: Routledge & Kegan Paul).

Hartup, W. (1968), 'Early education and childhood socialisation', *Journal of Research and Development in Education*, vol. 1, pp. 16–29.

Haynes, H., White, B., and Held, R. (1965), 'Visual accommodation in human infants', *Science*, vol. 148, pp. 528–30.

Himmelweit, H., and Swift, B. (1969), 'A model for the understanding of the school as a socialising agent', in *Trends and Issues in Developmental Psychology*, ed. P. Mussen, J. Langer and M. Covington (New York: Holt, Rinehart & Winston), pp. 154–80.

Hoffman, M. (1975), 'Moral internalisation, parental power and the nature of child–parent interaction', *Developmental Psychology*, vol. 11, pp. 228–39.

Hoffman, M. (1976), 'Empathy, role-taking, guilt and development of altruistic motives', in *Moral Development and Behavior*, ed. T. Lickona (New York: Holt, Rinehart & Winston), pp. 124–43.

Hogan, R. (1973), 'Moral conduct and moral character', *Psychological Bulletin*, vol. 79, pp. 217–32.

Hoyle, E. (1969), *The Role of the Teacher* (London: Routledge & Kegan Paul).

Hutt, C., and Hutt, S. (1970), *Direct Observation and Measurement of Behavior* (Springfield, Ill.: C. C. Thomas).

Jackson, P. (1968), *Life in Classrooms* (New York: Holt, Rinehart & Winston).

Jones, E., Roch, L., Shaver, K., Goethals, G., and Ward, L. (1968), 'Pattern performance and ability attribution: an unexpected primacy effect', *Journal of Personality and Social Psychology*, vol. 10, pp. 317–41.

Kelley, G. A. (1955), *The Psychology of Personal Constructs* (New York: Norton).

Kemp, L. (1955), 'Attainment in primary schools; environmental and other characteristics determining', *British Journal of Educational Psychology*, vol. 25, pp. 67–77.

Kerlinger, F. (1973), *Foundations of Behavioural Research* (London: Holt, Rinehart & Winston).

Kohlberg, L. (1969), 'The cognitive developmental approach to socialization', in *Handbook of Socialization: Theory and Research*, ed. D. Goslin (Chicago: Rand McNally), pp. 347–480.

Kohlberg, L. (1976), 'Moral stages and moralisation', in *Moral Development and Behavior*, ed. T. Lickona (New York: Holt, Rinehart & Winston), pp. 31–53.

Kounin, J. (1970), *Discipline and Group Management in Classrooms* (London: Holt, Rinehart & Winston).

Krosier, K., and DeVault, V. (1967), 'Effects of teacher personality', *Psychology in Schools*, vol. 4, pp. 40–4.

Kutnick, P. (1974), 'The inception of social authority; a comparative study of samples of children aged 4–12 in England and midwestern United States', PhD thesis, University of London, Institute of Education.

Kutnick, P., and Brees, P. (1982), 'The development of cooperation; explorations in cognitive and moral competence and social authority', *British Journal of Educational Psychology* (in press).

Labov, W. (1973), 'The logic of nonstandard English', in *Tinker, Tailor . . . the Myth of Cultural Deprivation*, ed. N. Keddie (Harmondsworth: Penguin), pp. 21–66.

Lacey, C. (1970), *Hightown Grammar* (Manchester: Manchester University Press).

Lawick-Goodall, J. van (1976), 'Early tool using in wild chimpanzees', in *Play*, ed. J. Bruner, A. Jolly and K. Sylva (Harmondsworth: Penguin), pp. 222–5.

Lickona, T. (1980), 'Beyond justice: a curriculum for cooperation', in *Practical Dimensions of Moral Education*, ed. D. Cochrane and M. Manley-Casimir (New York: Praeger).

Livesley, W., and Bromley, D. (1967), *Person Perception in Childhood and Adolescence* (London: Wiley).

Livingstone, R. (1941), *The Future of Education* (Cambridge: Cambridge University Press).

Loevinger, J. (1976), *Ego Development* (San Francisco: Jossey-Bass).

McCandless, B., Bilores, C., and Bennett, H. (1961), 'Peer popularity and dependence on adults in preschool socialisation', *Child Development*, vol. 32, pp. 511–18.

McGurk, H. (1974), 'Visual perception in young infants', in *New Perspectives in Child Development*, ed. B. Foss (Harmondsworth: Penguin), pp. 11–52.

Magowan, S., and Lee, T. (1970), 'Some sources of error in the use of the projective method for the measurement of moral judgement', *British Journal of Psychology*, vol. 61, pp. 535–43.

Marsh, P., Rosser, E., and Harré, R. (1978), *The Rules of Disorder* (London: Routledge & Kegan Paul).

Mead, G. H. (1964), *On Social Psychology* (Chicago: Phoenix Books).

Millar, W. S. (1974), 'Conditioning and learning in early infancy', in *New Perspec-*

tives in Child Development, ed. B. Foss (Harmondsworth: Penguin), pp. 53–84.

Mitchell, S., and Shepard, M. (1966), 'Children's behaviour, a comparison of at home and at school', *British Journal of Educational Psychology*, vol. 36, pp. 248–54.

Morrison, A., and McIntyre, D. (1969), *Teachers and Teaching* (Harmondsworth: Penguin).

Murray, H., Herling, G., and Staebler, B. (1972), 'The effects of locus of control and pattern of performances of teachers' evaluations of a student', paper presented at the American Psychological Association convention.

Musgrove, F., and Taylor, P. (1969), *Society and the Teacher's Role* (London: Routledge & Kegan Paul).

Mussen, P., and Eisenberg-Berg, N. (1977), *Roots of Caring, Sharing and Helping* (San Francisco: Freeman).

Nardine, F. (1971), 'The development of competence', in *Psychology and Educational Practice*, ed. G. S. Lesser (Glenview, Ill.: Scott Foresman).

Nash, R. (1973), *Classrooms Observed* (London: Routledge & Kegan Paul).

Nash, R. (1976), *School Learning* (London: Methuen).

Piaget, J. (1928), *Judgement and Reasoning* (London: Routledge & Kegan Paul).

Piaget, J. (1959), *The Language and Thought of the Child* (London: Routledge & Kegan Paul).

Piaget, J. (1962), *Play, Dreams and Imitation* (London: Routledge & Kegan Paul).

Piaget, J. (1965), *Moral Judgement of the Child* (New York: The Free Press).

Piaget, J. (1971), *Science of Education and Psychology of the Child* (New York: Longman).

Piaget, J., and Inhelder, B. (1969), *The Psychology of the Child* (London: Routledge & Kegan Paul).

Pickering, G. (1969), *The Challenge to Education* (Harmondsworth: Penguin).

Plato [1961], *Republic*, trans. P. Shorey, in *The Collected Dialogues of Plato*, ed. E. Hamilton and H. Cairnes (Princeton, NJ: Princeton University Press).

Plowden Commission (1967), *Children and Their Primary Schools* (London: HMSO).

Rosen, H. (1972), *Language and Class* (Bristol: Falling Wall Press).

Rosenshine, B., and Furst, N. (1973), 'The use of direct observation to study teaching', in *Second Handbook of Research on Teaching*, ed. M. Travers (Chicago: Rand McNally), pp. 122–83.

Rosenthal, R., and Jacobson, L. (1968), *Pygmalion in the Classroom* (New York: Holt, Rinehart & Winston).

Rousseau, J. (1911), *Emile*, trans. B. Foxley (London: Dent).

Rubin, K. (1973), 'Egocentrism in childhood: a unitary concept?', *Child Development*, vol. 44, pp. 102–10.

Russell, B. (1951), 'The functions of a teacher', in *Unpopular Essays* (London: Allen & Unwin).

Rutter, M., Maughan, B., Mortimore, P., Ouston, J., and Smith, A. (1979), *Fifteen Thousand Hours. Secondary Schools and Their Effects on Children* (London: Open Books).

Schaffer, H. R. (1971), *The Growth of Sociability* (Harmondsworth: Penguin).

Seaver, W. (1971), 'Effects of naturally induced expectancies of the academic performances of pupils in primary grades', PhD thesis, University of Illinois.

Selman, R. (1976a), 'A structural-developmental analysis of interpersonal conceptions: peer relations concepts in poorly adjusted and well adjusted preadolescents', in *Tenth Annual Minnesota Symposium on Child Development*, ed. A. Pick (Minneapolis, Minn.: University of Minnesota Press), pp. 156–200.

Selman, R. (1976b), 'Social-cognitive understanding', in *Moral Development and Behavior*, ed. T. Lickona (New York: Holt, Rinehart & Winston), pp. 299–316.

Shantz, C. (1975), 'The development of social cognition', in *Review of Child Development Research*, ed. E. M. Hetherington (Chicago: University of Chicago Press), pp. 257–324.

Sharp, R., and Green, A. (1976), *Education and Social Control* (London: Routledge & Kegan Paul).

Simon, A., and Boyer, E. (eds) (1970), *Mirrors for Behavior* (Philadelphia, Pa: Classroom Interaction Newsletter).

Smith, P. (1974), 'Ethological methods', in *New Perspectives in Child Development*, ed. B. Foss (Harmondsworth: Penguin), pp. 85–137.

Stayton, D., Hogan, R., and Ainsworth, M. (1971), 'Infant obedience and maternal behavior: origins of socialisation reconsidered', *Child Development*, vol. 42, pp. 1057–69.

Stern, D. (1977), *The First Relationship: Infant and Mother* (London: Fontana/Open Books).

Stubbs, M. (1976), *Language, Schools and Classrooms* (London: Methuen).

Stubbs, M., and Delamont, S. (eds) (1976), *Explorations in Classroom Observation* (London: Wiley).

Thompson, E. P. (1963), *The Making of the English Working Class* (Harmondsworth: Penguin).

Thompson, S. K. (1975), 'Gender labels and early sex role development', *Child Development*, vol. 46, pp. 339–47.

Tibble, J. (1967), 'The development of the study of education', in *The Study of Education*, ed. J. Tibble (London: Routledge & Kegan Paul), pp. 1–28.

Trevarthan, C. (1975), 'Early attempts at speech', in *Child Alive*, ed. R. Lewin (London: Temple Smith), pp. 62–80.

Turiel, E. (1969), 'Development of processes in the child's moral thinking', in *Trends and Issues in Developmental Psychology*, ed. P. Mussen, J. Langer and M. Covington (New York: Holt, Rinehart & Winston).

Vaizey, J. (1967), *Education in the Modern World* (London: Weidenfeld & Nicolson).

Vygotsky, L. (1966), *Thought and Language* (Cambridge, Mass.: MIT Press).

Vygotsky, L. (1967), 'Play and its role in the mental development of the child', *Soviet Psychology*, vol. 5, pp. 6–18.

White, R. (1960), 'Competence and the psychosexual stages of development', in *Nebraska Symposium on Motivation*, ed. M. R. Jones (Lincoln, Nebr.: University of Nebraska Press), pp. 97–141.

Whitehead, A. (1964), *The Aims of Education* (New York: New America Library).

Wickman, E. (1928), *Children's Behavior and Teachers' Attitudes* (Worcester: The Commonwealth Fund).

Wilcox, B. (1969), 'Visual preferences of human infants for representations of the human face', *Journal of Experimental Child Psychology*, vol. 7, pp. 10–20.

Willis, P. (1977), *Learning to Labour* (Farnborough: Saxon House).

Wilson, B. (1962), 'The teacher's role: a sociological analysis', *British Journal of Sociology*, vol. 13, pp. 15–32.

Wohlwill, J. (1973), *The Study of Behavioral Development* (New York: Academic Press).

Wood, M. (1968), 'A study of children's growing social and motivational awareness', PhD thesis, University of London, Institute of Education.

Wright, D. (1962), 'A comparative study of the adolescent's concepts of parents and teachers', *Educational Review*, vol. 14, pp. 226–32.

Yando, R., and Kagan, J. (1968), 'The effect of teacher tempo on the child', *Child Development*, vol. 39, pp. 27–34.

Yee, A. (1968), 'Source and direction of causal influence in teacher–pupil relationships', *Journal of Educational Psychology*, vol. 59, pp. 275–82.

Youniss, J. (1978), 'The nature of social development: a conceptual discussion of cognition', in *Issues in Childhood Social Development*, ed. H. McGurk (London: Methuen), pp. 203–27.

Youniss, J. (1980), *Parents and Peers in Social Development* (Chicago: University of Chicago Press).

Index

Thompson, E. P. 40, *122*
Thompson, S. K. 18, *122*
three mountains 26–7
Tibble, J. 36, *122*
tool 16
tradition 37
transmission of knowledge 35, 46
of culture 36, 47
Trevarthan, C. 17, *122*
trust/dependence xi, 11, 12, 31, 83, 87, 90, 93, 98, 99, 104
Turiel, E. 54, *122*

Vaizey, J. 36, *122*
validity 59, 61, 63
verbal awareness 60–2

vocabulary 18
Vygotsky, L. 18, 26, 98, *122*

White, R. 17, *122*
Whitehead, A. 35, *122*
Wickman, E. 50, *122*
Wilcox, B. M. 10, *122*
Willis, P. 50, *122*
Wilson, B. 40, *122*
Wishart, J. G. 10, *117*
Wohlwill, J. 57, 61, 94, *122*
Wood, M. 65, 78, 79, *122*
Wright, D. 48, 50, *122*

Yando, R. and Kagan, J. 46, 57, *122*
Yee, A. 43, *122*
Youniss, J. 33, 54, 60, 91, *122–23*